Contemporary
Diagnosis and Management of

Common Psychiatric Disorders®

Eric Hollander, MD
Professor of Psychiatry
Mount Sinai School of Medicine
New York, NY

and

Cheryl M. Wong, MD
Assistant Professor
Mount Sinai School of Medicine
New York, NY

Published by Handbooks in Health Care Co.,
Newtown, Pennsylvania, USA

This book has been prepared and is presented as a service to the medical community. The information provided reflects the knowledge, experience, and personal opinions of Eric Hollander, MD, Professor of Psychiatry, Mount Sinai School of Medicine, New York, NY, and Cheryl M. Wong, MD, Assistant Professor, Mount Sinai School of Medicine, New York, NY.

This book is not intended to replace or to be used as a substitute for the complete prescribing information prepared by each manufacturer for each drug. Because of possible variations in drug indications, in dosage information, in newly described toxicities, in drug/drug interactions, and in other items of importance, reference to such complete prescribing information is definitely recommended before any of the drugs discussed are used or prescribed.

International Standard Book Number: 1-884065-42-2

Library of Congress Catalog Card Number: 98-71700

Table of Contents

Section I:
Overview and General Principles

Chapter 1

Introduction

Anxiety and depression are two of the most common disorders in medicine. Although they cause substantial morbidity and mortality, they largely remain underdiagnosed and undertreated. The National Institute of Mental Health estimates that more than 23 million people a year in the United States are affected by an anxiety disorder, and that 10 million are affected by depression. The economic toll of these illnesses includes treatment costs, loss of productivity, and costs from illness or death. Estimates of the economic burden from depression in the United States reach $43.7 billion ($12.4 billion in treatment costs, $7.5 billion in mortality costs, and $23.8 billion in morbidity costs). In fact, depression has a greater impact than other chronic medical conditions such as hypertension, diabetes, arthritis, and lung disease, as measured by physical, role, and social functioning, perceived current health, and bodily pain experienced.

Depression and anxiety disorders can substantially affect quality of life as well. For example, patients with generalized anxiety disorder and panic disorder describe significant impairment to their daily lives. A related illness, obsessive-compulsive disorder, profoundly affects psychosocial functioning by damaging relationships with a spouse and children, and by resulting in job loss.

Because most patients with these disorders are treated by primary care physicians, helping these clinicians to identify symptoms, to correctly diagnose anxiety and depressive disorders, and to appropriately treat these patients is critical. This informed care would significantly improve function, quality of life, and overall medical health of patients who suffer from these disorders. Most physicians understand that many patients with depressive or anxiety disorders often do not verbalize their feelings, but rather present with somatic complaints. Therefore, clinicians must openly address these issues with their patients and help remove the stigma associated with these disorders.

The symptoms of anxiety and depression should raise suspicions and prompt clinicians to uncover the actual associated disorders and syndromes. If correctly treated, symptoms can be dramatically reduced. However, anxiety and depression do not represent a homogenous group of disorders. Consequently, appropriate diagnosis is the first step to tailoring effective treatment for each patient.

Diagnoses of Depression

To screen a patient for depression, ask him or her the following questions:
- Do you often feel down or blue?
- Are your sleep and appetite decreased or increased?
- Do you feel run down and tired most of the time?
- Do you often feel hopeless and helpless?
- Do you often think about death and suicide?

Determining the exact depressive disorder is important; for example, a patient may have a major depressive disorder or depression caused by alcoholism that had not been previously diagnosed. Determination of the patient's suicidality and level of danger is critical. Importantly, patients who suddenly 'recover' from a depression may be at great risk for attempting suicide because they may see ending life as a resolution, leading to their sudden calm.

The next step is to exclude medical conditions or substance use that can cause depression, and to treat the underlying problem. An example is a patient who presents with all the signs and symptoms of a major depression on medical work-up and who has a high thyroid-stimulating hormone (TSH) and low triiodothyronine (T_3) and thyroxine (T_4) levels. After appropriate thyroid replacement therapy, the patient's depressive symptoms gradually resolve.

The next most important step is to differentially determine whether the patient has a purely depressive disorder or a bipolar (manic-depressive) diathesis, because antidepressants often cause bipolar patients to cycle into a manic or hypomanic episode. The more difficult cases include those patients who present with depression but not manic or hypomanic episodes, and who have a strong family history of bipolar disorder. These patients require more careful monitoring for emergence of manic symptoms.

The next step is to determine if a patient exhibits symptoms of psychosis, such as hearing voices when other people are not in the room, or seeing things that other people do not see. These abnormalities indicate that the patient may need treatment with antipsychotic medication.

Clinicians then must determine the duration and severity of the depressive episodes, whether they are recurrent, and how they interfere with a patient's function. Also, the clinician should ask about a family history of mood disorders and suicide attempts, because these increase a patient's risk of morbidity and mortality.

Diagnoses of Anxiety

To screen a patient for anxiety, ask him or her the following questions:
- Do you often feel tense or keyed up?
- Do you worry a great deal or feel irritable?
- Do you get palpitations or shortness of breath?
- Do you often have muscle aches or feelings of weakness?
- Do you have repetitive disturbing thoughts or habits?

Once again, after the presence of anxiety has been established, exclusion of medical or substance-induced causes is important. Both substance intoxication and withdrawal can induce anxiety symptoms. It is also important to ask if the patient has been taking over-the-counter medications such as diet preparations or herbal remedies that can, in fact, lead to anxiety symptoms. Determining whether the anxiety occurs constantly or in episodes, how long the anxiety lasts, and the precipitating or associated factors are all important. Mood disorders often have an anxiety component; thus, they must be included in the differential. The presence of obsessions or compulsions also is important to determine, as are symptoms of impulse control and arousal associated with anxiety.

Both depression and anxiety are often associated with self-medication with alcohol, drugs, or smoking. In addition, certain medical conditions are more highly associated with comorbid depression and anxiety. These include human immunodeficiency virus (HIV) infection, pregnancy, cerebrovascular accidents, myocardial infarction, certain cancers, and thyroid conditions.

Specific anxiety and depressive disorders respond differently to different treatments. This handbook concentrates mainly on the different pharmacotherapies and biologic treatments available for these disorders. In addition, assessment and diagnostic criteria are outlined. The disorders are divided into anxiety- or depression-related. Each disorder commonly encountered by primary care physicians is described, and insights into appropriate treatment and therapy for each population are presented.

We begin by describing and providing profiles for different medications and other biologic treatments for anxiety and depression as a basis for selection of the appropriate agent. The same biologic agent often can treat both anxiety and depression.

Selected Readings

Greenberg PE, Stiglin LE, Finkelstein SN, et al: The economic burden of depression in 1990. *J Clin Psychiatry* 1993;54:405-418.

Hales RE, Yudofsky SC, Talbott JA, eds. *The American Psychiatric Press Textbook of Psychiatry*, 2nd ed. Washington, DC, American Psychiatric Press, 1994.

Halleck SL: *Evaluation of the Psychiatric Patient: A Primer*. New York, Plenum, 1991.

Hollander E, Simeon D, Gorman JM: Anxiety disorders. In: Hales RE, Yudofsky SC, Talbott JA, eds. *The American Psychiatric Press Textbook of Psychiatry*, 2nd ed. Washington, DC, American Psychiatric Press, 1994.

Hollander E, Stein DJ, Kwon J, et al: Psychological function and economic costs of obsessive-compulsive disorder. *CNS Spectrums* 1997;210:16-25.

Jefferson JW, Greist JH: Mood disorders. In: Hales RE, Yudofsky SC, Talbott JA, eds. *The American Psychiatric Press Textbook of Psychiatry*, 2nd ed. Washington, DC, American Psychiatric Press, 1994.

Liebowitz MR, Hollander E, Schneier F, et al: Anxiety and depression: discrete diagnostic entities? *J Clin Psychopharmacol* 1990;10:61S-66S.

Massion AO, Warshaw MG, Keller MB: Quality of life and psychiatric morbidity in panic disorder and generalized anxiety disorder. *Am J Psychiatry* 1993;150:600-607.

Wells KB, Rogers W, Burnam A, et al: How the medical comorbidity of depressed patients differs across health care settings: results from the Medical Outcomes Study. *Am J Psychiatry* 1991; 148:1688-1696.

Wells KB, Stewart A, Hays RD, et al: The functioning and well-being of depressed patients. Results from the Medical Outcomes Study. *JAMA* 1989;262:914-919.

Chapter **2**

Pharmacotherapy and Other Biologic Treatments

D epression and anxiety both involve the neurotransmitter systems in the brain. Consequently, drugs used for treating depression and anxiety mostly affect the three major neurotransmitter systems: serotonin, norepinephrine, and gamma-aminobutyric acid (GABA) systems. However, the drugs may also work on other neurotransmitters, such as acetylcholine and histamine, and the exact receptors and neurotransmitter systems that each medication affects determine its side effect profile.

Antidepressants

Although the following classes of drugs are widely known as antidepressants, they are effective in treating a range of psychiatric and medical illnesses and conditions. These include anxiety disorders, eating disorders, impulse-control disorders, personality disorders, enuresis, migraines, and pain management, in addition to depression.

Selective Serotonin Reuptake Inhibitors (SSRIs)

The selective serotonin reuptake inhibitors (SSRIs) were first introduced to the United States in 1988, after they were discovered in the 1970s. Since then, they have become widely used because of their more favorable side effect profile when compared with that of the older antidepressants.

Table 1: Significant Inhibition of Cytochrome P-450 Isozymes by SSRIs, SNRIs, and Atypicals

SSRI	Isozyme			
	3A4	2D6	1A2	2C9
fluoxetine	+	+++	+	++
norfluoxetine*	++/+++	+++	+	++
sertraline	+	+	+	+
desmethylsertraline*	+	+	+	+
paroxetine	+	+++	+	+
fluvoxamine	++	+	+++	++
citalopram	-	+	+	+
Other 5-HT Active Antidepressants				
venlafaxine	-	+	-	-
mirtazapine	-	-	-	-
nefazodone	+++	+	-	-

+: mild; ++: moderate; +++: strong inhibition of isozyme; - : no significant effect

* inactive metabolite

All SSRIs are well absorbed orally, reaching peak effect in 4 to 8 hours, and are hepatically metabolized. Different SSRIs inhibit different cytochrome P-450 isozymes (Table 1). They have different potencies and half-lives (Table 2), and do not have significant direct effects on the norepinephrine, dopamine, acetylcholine, and histamine systems. Consequently, they have a favorable side effect profile.

Dosage: SSRIs may be taken with food to decrease GI complaints. When treatment is initiated, doses can be divided to decrease side effects, and then can be switched to daily dosing if tolerated. Depending on whether the SSRI activates or sedates a person, the daily dose can be taken in the morning or before bedtime (Table 3). Because children and the elderly are more sensitive to medication effects, the therapeutic dosage range for them is usually lower than for young adults.

Overdose: SSRIs are safer than other antidepressants when taken in overdose. The rate of lethality with SSRI overdose alone is very low. Overdose symptoms include agitation, tremor, vomiting, tachycardia, hypertension, hyperthermia, ocular oscillations, myoclonic jerks, insomnia, restlessness, and seizures. However, a potential danger with SSRIs is the serotonin syndrome, which can occur with concurrent use of other serotonergic medications such as monoamine oxidase inhibitors (MAOIs), L-tryptophan, and sumatriptan (Imitrex®).

Drug Discontinuation: A discontinuation syndrome has been described with the SSRIs, especially those with shorter half-lives. Symptoms include dizziness, lightheadedness, insomnia, headache, and sensory disturbance. The syndrome may last up to 3 weeks, but may be alleviated by restarting the antidepressant or starting an antidepressant with a similar pharmacologic profile. To avoid this syndrome, SSRIs should be gradually tapered.

Drug Interactions: Concomitant use of SSRIs and MAOIs and other serotonergic agents can lead to the potentially fatal serotonin syndrome (see *Overdose*). There should be a 2-week washout period between the discontinuation of an MAOI and the start of an SSRI, at least a 4-week interval between stopping an SSRI and starting an MAOI, and 6 weeks for fluoxetine (Prozac®). SSRIs can be administered with cyclic antidepressants, but tend to raise their levels because of inhibition of the P-450 isoenzymes 2D6 and 3A4. Therefore, small doses of cyc-

Table 2: Pharmacokinetics and Potency Profiles of SSRI

Medication	5-HT Inhibition Potency*	Peak Concentration From Initial Dose	t 1/2 (hours)
fluvoxamine (Luvox®)	25	2-8 hours	15 hours
fluoxetine (Prozac®)	6	4-8 hours	84 hours
paroxetine (Paxil®)	7	3-8 hours	21 hours
sertraline (Zoloft®)	1	6-10 hours	26 hours
citalopram (Celexa™)	1	3-4 hours	35 hours

* Lower numbers denote more potent serotonin agents.

lic antidepressants should be used, and their levels should be monitored. Because SSRIs are hepatically metabolized and have a range of protein binding, they have clinically important interactions with other medications (Table 4).

Adverse Effects: Side effects of SSRIs include gastrointestinal (GI) disturbances (eg, nausea, diarrhea, anorexia, dyspepsia), headache, nervousness, insomnia, anxiety, and drowsiness, and a low incidence (<0.2%) for the development of seizures. They can also impair sexual functioning (eg, anorgasmia, delayed ejaculation), which may respond to yohimbine (Yocon®), cyproheptadine (Periactin®), perhaps sildenafil (Viagra®), or stimulants such as dextroamphetamine (Dexedrine®). SSRIs can also

Steady State Reached After:	Active Metabolites	Protein Binding
10 days	none	77%
2-4 weeks	norfluoxetine	95%
4-14 days	none	95%
10-14 days	dexmethylsertraline	>97%
1-2 weeks	10% active — didemethylcitalopram — demethylcitalopram	80%

cause hypoglycemia; therefore, diabetic patients should be carefully monitored. In addition, cases of hyponatremia have occurred, especially with patients concurrently taking diuretics. SSRIs can also cause akathisia (anxiety and restlessness), and parkinson-like movement disorders such as tremor, especially when taken in combination with antipsychotics or dopaminergic medications. Because SSRIs are hepatically metabolized, they should be used carefully in hepatically compromised patients.

Generally, clinicians should avoid prescribing any medication for pregnant patients, although some SSRIs have been studied in pregnancy, and have been found to have no significant adverse effects on newborns. Because

Table 3: Dosage Forms and Ranges of SSRIs

SSRI	Forms Available	Adult Dosage Range	Titration
fluvoxamine (Luvox®)	25-, 50-, 100-mg tabs	50-300 mg/d	50 mg/week
fluoxetine (Prozac®)	10-, 20-mg caps 20 mg/5 mL liquid	10-80 mg/d	10-20 mg/week
paroxetine (Paxil®)	10-, 20-, 30-, 40-mg tabs 10 mg/5 mL liquid	10-60 mg/d	10-20 mg/week
sertraline (Zoloft®)	25-, 50-, 100-mg tabs 50 mg/5 mL liquid	50-200 mg/d	50 mg/week
citalopram (Celexa™)	20-, 40-mg tabs	20-60 mg/d	20 mg/week

SSRIs are excreted in breast milk, breast-feeding should be avoided.

Serotonin-Norepinephrine Reuptake Inhibitors (SNRIs)

This class of medications stimulates (blocks reuptake of) both the serotonin and norepinephrine systems. Venlafaxine (Effexor® and Effexor® XR) also inhibits reuptake of dopamine, and mirtazapine (Remeron®) is a 5-HT receptor antagonist, in addition to blocking reuptake.

Venlafaxine

Venlafaxine is available in both acute-dosing and sustained-release forms, the former requiring b.i.d.-t.i.d. dosing, and the latter needed only once a day. It is hepatically metabolized, has at least one active metabolite, and is renally cleared. It is a relatively weak inhibitor of the cytochrome P-450 2D6 isozyme. However, drugs that inhibit the cytochrome P-450 system, such as paroxetine (Paxil®), sertraline (Zoloft®), fluoxetine (Prozac®), fluvoxamine (Luvox®), and citalopram (Celexa™), may increase venlafaxine levels. Venlafaxine has a half-life of about 5 hours, and its active metabolite has a half-life of about 11 hours. It reaches steady state in about 3 days in young healthy adults. It does not act on muscarinic, histaminic, or alpha-adrenergic receptors. It is available in 37.5-mg, 75-mg, and 150-mg sustained-release capsules (XR forms), and 25-mg, 37.5-mg, 50-mg, 75-mg, and 100-mg tablets, with the usual starting dose of 75 mg/d. The dose can be titrated by 75 mg/d every 1 to 2 weeks, but not faster than 75 mg every 4 days. The usual dosage range is 75 to 300 mg/d, with a maximum dose of 375 mg/d. Renally impaired patients should receive half the dose. Adverse effects include nausea, dry mouth, sedation, dizziness, nervousness, impaired sexual function (eg, abnormal orgasm, ejaculation, impotence), and increased blood pressure. The increase in blood pressure occurs more often in patients treated with more than 300 mg/d, and should be used cautiously in hypertensive patients. No studies have involved the use of venlafaxine in pregnant or nursing women. Venlafaxine should be stopped at least 2 weeks before initiating treatment with an MAOI.

Mirtazapine

Mirtazapine is well absorbed orally, metabolized hepatically, and cleared renally. Its elimination half-life is 20 to 40 hours. Side effects include sedation, increased appetite/weight gain, dizziness, and nausea, with a small risk of agranulocytosis, and a low incidence of anticholinergic and serotonergic effects. It has not been shown to decrease libido in clinical trials. Mirtazapine is available in 15-mg and 30-mg tablets, and the initial dose usually is

Table 4: Drug Interactions With SSRIs

SSRI	Other Drugs	Effect
fluvoxamine (Luvox®)	warfarin (Coumadin®) tricyclic antidepressants benzodiazepines calcium-channel blockers pimozide (Orap®) bupropion (Wellbutrin®) caffeine theophylline (Theo-Dur®) phenytoin (Dilantin®)	Raises drug level
	digoxin (Lanoxin®) atenolol (Tenormin®)	No effect
citalopram (Celexa™)	metoprolol (Lopressor®)	2-fold increase in drug level
	tricyclic antidepressants	Increases drug levels
	lithium	May increase serotonergic effects of citalopram
	cimetidine	Increases citalopram level
	carbamazepine (Tegretol®)	May cause increased clearance of citalopram
	digoxin	No effect
	warfarin	No effect

SSRI	Other Drugs	Effect
paroxetine (Paxil®)	tricyclic antidepressants	Raises drug level
	phenytoin	Raises drug level, lowers paroxetine level
	cimetidine (Tagamet®)	Raises paroxetine drug level
	digoxin propranolol warfarin	No effect
sertraline (Zoloft®)	tricyclic antidepressants	Raises drug level
	benzodiazepines	Decreases drug level
	calcium-channel blockers pimozide bupropion digoxin atenolol	No effect
fluoxetine (Prozac®)	tricyclic antidepressants carbamazepine (Tegretol®) benzodiazepines calcium-channel blockers bupropion pimozide phenytoin	Raises drug level
	warfarin digoxin	No effect

Table 5: Tricyclic Dosage Forms and Ranges

Tricyclic	Dosage Forms
imipramine (Tofranil®)	10-, 25-, 50-mg tabs 75-, 100-, 125-, 150-mg capsules 25-mg/2 mL parenteral
desipramine (Norpramin®)	10-, 25-, 50-, 75-, 100-, 150-mg tabs 25-, 50-mg capsules
amitriptyline (Elavil®)	10-, 25-, 50-, 75-, 100-, 150-mg tabs 10 mg/mL parenteral
nortriptyline (Pamelor®)	10-, 25-, 50-, 75-mg capsules 10 mg/5 mL liquid
clomipramine (Anafranil®)	25-, 50-, 75-mg caps

15 to 30 mg/d administered in a single daily dose, preferably in the evening before bedtime. The effective dose range is 15 to 45 mg/d.

Tricyclic Antidepressants (TCAs)

All the tricyclic antidepressants (TCAs) are available in oral form; some are available as parenterals, although this form is not often clinically used. Oral preparations

Adult Dosage Range	Therapeutic Level	Titration Rate
50-300 mg/d	>225 ng/mL (imipramine + desipramine)	50 mg/ 4-5 days
50-300 mg/d	>125 ng/mL	25 mg/ 4-5 days
50-300 mg/d	>120 ng/mL (amitriptyline + nortriptyline)	50 mg/ 4-5 days
25-150 mg/d	50-150 ng/mL	25 mg/ 4-5 days
50-250 mg/d	<800 ng/mL	50 mg/week

are rapidly absorbed with a large first-pass effect. TCAs are hepatically metabolized by the P-450 system, with many parent compounds giving rise to active metabolites. Tricyclics cross the blood-brain barrier well, and all are highly protein bound; therefore, they cannot be removed by hemodialysis. The elimination course is biphasic, with about half the dose removed after 48 to 72 hours, and the other half excreted over the next few weeks.

Because of the potential cardiac side effects of TCAs, patients must be screened carefully before receiving one. The presence of any cardiac conduction disease is a contraindication for TCA use. All candidates over age 40 should receive a screening electrocardiogram (EKG). No other tests are indicated in healthy adults before starting TCA therapy.

Tricyclics are started at a low dose (equivalent to 50 mg/d of imipramine [Tofranil®]), and titrated up gradually, by about 50 mg/d every 4 to 5 days as side effects allow, to a dosage range of 150 to 300 mg/d of imipramine (Table 5). TCAs are generally administered in a single dose before bedtime because of their sedating side effects. If the patient still does not optimally respond after 3 or 4 weeks, the dose should be again titrated up as side effects allow. The maximum dose of tricyclics is equivalent to 300 mg/d of imipramine. The trial is only considered a failure if the patient does not adequately respond after 4 to 6 weeks of treatment at the maximum dosage. Drug levels can also be followed during therapy. Imipramine and desipramine (Norpramin®) have a linear relationship between blood levels and clinical improvement. Patients whose combined imipramine/desipramine (IMI/DMI) level on imipramine of 225 ng/mL and 125 ng/mL for those on desipramine tend to do better clinically than those patients with lower levels. Nortriptyline (Pamelor®) has a blood level range of 50 to 150 ng/mL, outside of which the patient's response is much less robust. Studies of amitriptyline (Elavil®) levels have been unclear about the utility of levels, with linear, nonlinear, and lack of relationship reported by different investigators.

Discontinuation: To discontinue a tricyclic for any reason, the medication should be gradually tapered over a few weeks, rather than abruptly stopped, because withdrawal symptoms can occur. These include vomiting, nausea, diarrhea, headache, fatigue, malaise, sleep abnormalities, akathisia, and parkinsonism, and paradoxic behavior resulting in hypomanic or manic symptoms. Symptoms may occur as early as 12 hours after a missed TCA dose, but withdrawal phenomena usually occur 24 to 48 hours after the last dose. Symptoms can continue for as long as a month.

Side Effects: Side effects of the tricyclics are related to their anticholinergic effects (dry mouth, constipation, urinary hesitancy, and blurred vision) and alpha-adrenergic effects (orthostatic hypotension). Desipramine and nortriptyline have fewer side effects compared with other TCAs. TCAs also have quinidine-like effects on cardiac conduction, including intracardiac conduction slowing. In fact, the chief medical contraindication to the use of tricyclics is cardiac conduction disturbances such as bifascicular block, left bundle branch block, and prolonged QT interval. TCAs can lower the seizure threshold, and cause sedation and weight gain. Most importantly, overdose may be lethal. Most side effects increase with dose escalation. The elderly generally are more susceptible to side effects. Tricyclics also can cause sexual dysfunction in men and women. This is usually dose-related.

Overdose: Acute overdoses of more than 1,000 mg of a tricyclic compound are usually toxic, and potentially fatal. Death may result from cardiac arrhythmia, hypotension, or intractable seizures. Serum levels of more than 1,000 ng/mL, and increased QRS intervals to 0.10 seconds or greater, both represent a serious overdose. Most symptoms develop within 24 hours of an acute overdose, although cardiac effects do not peak for 48 to 72 hours. Management of overdose includes intubation or induction of emesis, and gastric lavage with activated charcoal with a cathartic. Because tricyclics are highly protein bound, hemodialysis is not effective. Patients with a serious overdose require cardiac monitoring. Digoxin, quinidine, procainamide, and disopyramide should be avoided because they may precipitate heart block.

Drug Interactions: Drugs that have CNS depressant effects (eg, alcohol, antihistamines, antipsychotics, benzodiazepines) can worsen sedation when taken with tricyclics. Drugs that can worsen hypotension include diuretics, alpha-adrenergic blockers such as clonidine (Catapres®), and beta-adrenergic blockers such as propranolol (Inderal®). Anticholinergic effects can be increased by antihistamines, antiparkinsonian medications, over-the-counter sleeping preparations, and antidiarrheals. In addition, tricyclics can increase the effects of warfarin (Coumadin®) and block the effects of guanethidine (Ismelin®). Tricyclics are metabolized by the P-450 isozymes 2D6 and 3A4 and, therefore, any inhibitor of these systems, such as SSRIs and nefazodone (Serzone®), can increase the level of the tricyclic. Tricyclic levels can also be affected by other medications (Table 6).

Monoamine Oxidase Inhibitors (MAOIs)

This class of drugs is generally accepted as effective as the other antidepressants. However, MAOIs are less commonly used as first-line agents because lack of adherence to dietary precautions can lead to hypertensive crisis, and because of safety issues associated with overdose. Of the four most common MAOIs, three—phenelzine (Nardil®), tranylcypromine (Parnate®), and isocarboxazid (Marplan®)—are all nonspecific inhibitors of MAOa and MAOb, and the fourth, selegiline (Eldepryl®, Atapryl™), is a specific inhibitor of MAOb. Two hydrazine-derived MAOIs, isocarboxazid and phenelzine, are hepatically acetylated, leading to greater side effects in slow acetylators, which comprises about half of North American and European populations, and more than half of Asian populations. The levels of tranylcypromine, unlike the hydrazine MAOIs, correlate with its hypotensive effects. The onset of antidepressant effect of MAOIs is 2 to 4 weeks, although maximum inhibition of MAO occurs in several days. Discontinuation

Table 6: Selected Drug Interactions With Tricyclic Levels

Increase TCA Levels	Decrease TCA Levels
amphetamines	chronic alcohol use
antipsychotics	barbiturates
oral contraceptives	carbamazepine (Tegretol®)
disulfiram (Antabuse®)	phenytoin (Dilantin®)
glucocorticoids	rifampin (Rifadin®)
SSRIs	chronic tobacco use
thiazides	
thyroid hormone	

of MAOIs results in restoration of enzyme activity in about 2 weeks.

MAOIs interact with tyramine and other amines by increasing uptake of vasoactive amines by the sympathetic system because of decreased breakdown. This results in a noradrenergic crisis with severe hypertension, hyperpyrexia, tachycardia, diaphoresis, tremulousness, and cardiac arrhythmia. Therefore, tyramine and other vasoactive amine-containing foods should not be ingested by patients taking MAOIs. Interaction between MAOIs and other serotonergic medications can also lead to the serotonin syndrome (see *SSRIs: Overdose*).

Before beginning therapy with MAOIs, clinicians must educate patients about the risks of interactions with amine-containing foods, beverages, and medications. A list of restrictions is useful. Symptoms of hypertensive crisis should be described to patients, and patients should receive clear instructions to seek emergency medical atten-

Table 7: Dose Range and Titration of Selected MAOIs

Medication	Initial Dose	Titration
phenelzine (Nardil®)	15 mg b.i.d.-t.i.d.	15 mg/week
tranylcypromine (Parnate®)	10 mg b.i.d.-t.i.d.	10 mg/week

tion if they experience such adverse effects. A partial list of foods to avoid includes liver, fermented sausages, cured meats, caviar, cured or dried fish, avocados, fava beans, sauerkraut, yeast extracts such as Marmite and Bovril, Chianti wine, unfiltered beer, and cheeses *except* ricotta, cottage, and cream cheeses.

Initial dosing of MAOIs begins at low doses, with gradual titration, depending on side effects and desired effects (Table 7). Tolerance can occur to certain side effects, such as postural hypotension.

When discontinuing MAOIs, clinicians should taper the medications slowly over a week or so. Patients should not discontinue dietary restrictions until at least 14 days after discontinuation of the MAOI, because MAO levels do not immediately return to normal. Generally, a washout period of 2 weeks should occur between discontinuation of an MAOI and starting another antidepressant. Before switching to an MAOI, 2 weeks should pass after discontinuation of a tricyclic or SSRI, and 5 to 6 weeks for fluoxetine.

Side Effects: Side effects include postural hypotension, which is dose-related, and is worse in patients receiving concomitant diuretics or antihypertensives. CNS effects can occur, such as insomnia and agitation. Hyperadrenergic (hy-

Dose Range	In the Elderly
45-60 mg/d	begin 7.5 mg/d, range 30-60 mg/d
30-40 mg/d	begin 5 mg/d, range 30-40 mg/d

pertensive) crisis occurs with ingestion of tyramine-containing foods or sympathomimetic agents such as L-dopa and TCAs. Symptoms include irritability, severe hypertension, mydriasis, throbbing headache, diaphoresis, and nausea or vomiting. Treatment consists of alpha-adrenergic blockade with agents such as phentolamine (Regitine®) 5 mg IV, repeated as necessary. Calcium-channel blockers such as nifedipine (Procardia®, Adalat®) also can be used for mild to moderate reactions, although recent concerns have surfaced about increased risk of myocardial infarction with nifedipine. Beta-blockers should not be used because they tend to intensify vasoconstriction and worsen hypertension. Sexual side effects also can occur, including delayed ejaculation, impotence, and anorgasmia. Other side effects of MAOIs include substantial weight gain, anticholinergic side effects, and muscle twitching (which can be treated with vitamin B_6).

Overdose: MAOIs are dangerous in overdose. They circulate at low levels in the serum and are difficult to assay, so blood levels are not particularly useful. Symptoms of an overdose start about 12 hours after ingestion and peak at 24 hours after ingestion. Patients may be initially asymptomatic, but then experience hyperpyrexia and autonomic instability.

Atypical Antidepressants

These drugs are chemically unrelated to those already cited.

Trazodone

Trazodone (Desyrel®) inhibits serotonin reuptake, acts as a $5-HT_2$ antagonist, and may act as a serotomimetic substance, possibly through its chief metabolite, meta-chlorophenylpiperazine (m-CPP). The adverse effects of trazodone are mediated mostly through its alpha-adrenergic inhibition and its antihistaminergic activity. Trazodone is well absorbed orally, reaching peak levels by 2 hours. Its half-life is short, 6 to 11 hours, and it is excreted renally. Common side effects include sedation, orthostatic hypotension, nausea, and vomiting, all of which can be decreased by taking the medication in divided or bedtime doses, or with food. Trazodone lacks the quinidine-like cardiac effects of the TCAs, and it has rarely been associated with arrhythmias as well. Priapism (prolonged, painful erections) also is a rare side effect that can occur in both men and women, and patients should be advised to seek emergency care if this occurs. Trazodone is available in 50-mg, 100-mg, 150-mg, and 300-mg tablets. The usual adult dosage range is 200 to 600 mg/d for antidepressant effects, although doses as low as 50 mg/d have been used to target insomnia alone. Initially, a patient can be started on 50 mg/d and titrated up by 50 mg/d every 2 to 3 days, depending on the emergence of side effects and until the desired effects are achieved.

Nefazodone

Nefazodone (Serzone®) is chemically similar to trazodone, but with less alpha-adrenergic blockade and antihistaminergic activity, and possibly less risk for sedation and priapism. Nefazodone inhibits serotonin uptake, but also is a $5-HT_2$-postsynaptic blocker. The half-life of nefazodone is approximately 5 hours. It is a strong inhibitor of the P-450 isozyme 3A4 and a mild inhibitor of isozyme 2D6; therefore, it can increase levels of medications that are metabolized by these enzymes when taken concurrently, such as bupropion (Wellbutrin®) (3A4), pimozide (Orap®) (3A4), benzodiazepines, calcium-channel blockers (3A4), and TCAs (2D6, 3A4). The most common side effects are sedation, headache, dry mouth, and nausea. Nefazodone is available in 100-mg, 150-mg, and 200-mg tablets. The usual starting dose is 200 mg/d in divided doses, titrated by 100 mg/d each week, with a dosage range of 300 to 600 mg/d. Because the elderly are more sensitive to this medication, lower doses should be used.

Bupropion

Bupropion (Wellbutrin®, Wellbutrin® SR, Zyban®) is structurally related to amphetamine, and is a sympathomimetic agent. It acts on the dopaminergic and noradrenergic systems, and possibly to a lesser extent on the serotonergic system. It is well absorbed orally, hepatically metabolized, and renally excreted. It is metabolized by the P-450 isozyme 3A4. Therefore, its levels can be increased by concurrent use of fluoxetine, nefazodone, and, to a lesser extent, by sertraline and fluvoxamine (Luvox®). It reaches peak levels after about 2 hours, and has a half-life from 8 to 40 hours, with two active metabolites. The most common side effects include headache, insomnia, nausea, and upper respiratory complaints. Bupropion does not have alpha-adrenergic or anticholinergic effects, such as orthostatic hypotension and dry mouth. It does have a significantly increased risk for seizures at doses higher than 450 mg/d, below which the risk is about 0.4%, comparable to other antidepressants. The sustained-release form carries less seizure risk than the acute dosing form. Therefore, when taken in huge overdose or with mixed-drug overdose, the chance for the development of seizures,

Table 8: Common Benzodiazepines: Clinical Characteristics

Medication*	Equivalent Dose Potency (mg)
alprazolam (Xanax®)	0.5
clonazepam (Klonopin®)	0.25
chlordiazepoxide (Librium®)	10.0
diazepam (Valium®)	5.0
lorazepam (Ativan®)	1.0
temazepam (Restoril®)	30.0

* Oral route of administration.

bradycardia, and cardiac arrest is significant. The use of bupropion in pregnancy has not been studied and is not recommended. Bupropion is secreted in breast milk, so its use during nursing is not recommended. It should not be used with MAOIs because of the risk of hypertensive crisis. CNS toxicity also can occur when bupropion is taken with dopaminergic medications such as amantadine (Symmetrel®) and L-dopa.

Because bupropion is metabolized hepatically, levels of other hepatically metabolized drugs being taken concomitantly, such as carbamazepine (Tegretol®), cimetidine (Tagamet®), and phenytoin (Dilantin®), should be monitored more closely. Bupropion is available in immediate-release 75-mg and 100-mg tablets, which require b.i.d. dosing, in extended-release forms in 100-mg and 150-mg tablets (Wellbutrin® SR), and in 150-mg tablets (Zyban®), which require only once-a-day dosing. Initial adult doses should begin at about 150 mg/d and titrated not faster than 100 mg in 3 days because of the risk of seizures. The usual

Rate of Onset	Distribution	Elimination Half-Life (hours)
medium	intermediate	6-20; short-acting
medium	intermediate	18-50; long-acting
medium	slow	30-100; long-acting
fast	rapid	30-100; long-acting
medium	intermediate	10-20; short-acting
medium	rapid	8-20; short-acting

target dose is 300 mg/d, and the maximum dose should not be greater than 450 mg/d.

Anxiolytics

Benzodiazepines

Medications in this class are the most widely used in treating anxiety. They also have sedative, hypnotic, anticonvulsant, and muscle-relaxant properties. At lower doses they have anxiolytic effects; at higher doses, sedative-hypnotic effects. Benzodiazepines act on the GABA neurotransmitter system. Clinicians must be familiar with the pharmacology of this class of medications to prescribe them safely and effectively, and to prevent abuse. Physiologic dependence may develop with benzodiazepines, especially with long-term use of the more potent, shorter-acting drugs such as alprazolam (Xanax®) and lorazepam (Ativan®). However, drug *dependence*, which is manifested by physical withdrawal symptoms on drug cessa-

Table 9: Other Routes of Administration

Sublingual	lorazepam (Ativan®), alprazolam (Xanax®), triazolam (Halcion®)
Intramuscular (preferably in deltoid)	lorazepam, midazolam (Versed®)
Intravenous— given over 1-2 minutes, monitor blood pressure and respiration	diazepam (Valium®), lorazepam, midazolam

tion, is not the same as *addiction*, which is defined as emotional dependence on the drug. Also, benzodiazepines are cross-tolerant with alcohol. Therefore, benzodiazepines probably should not be prescribed for patients with a history of alcohol or drug abuse or dependence.

Most benzodiazepines are absorbed orally on an empty stomach. Many reach peak plasma levels in 1 to 3 hours; however, variation is wide. The rate of onset of action of the drug (Table 8) also affects a patient's experience; some describe the fast onset of action as a 'high,' or feel that the medication is therapeutic because they feel its effect more rapidly. Others, however, experience a fast onset as negative because of a dysphoric response or sedation. Apart from different potencies, all benzodiazepines have the same maximum effects (Table 8). Duration of effect (Table 8) depends on the distribution and half-life of each drug. Therefore, with short-term or single-dose use, absorption rates are important, and with chronic use, elimination rates determine which benzodiazepine suits a particular patient. In addition, interdose rebound anxiety and withdrawal problems occur more frequently with benzodiazepines with shorter half-lives.

Table 10: Dose Forms and Usual Adult Dosage Range

Medication	Dose Forms	Dosage Range (mg/d)
alprazolam (Xanax®)	0.25-, 0.5-, 1-, 2-mg tabs	0.5-8
temazepam (Restoril®)	15-, 30-mg tabs	15-30
lorazepam (Ativan®)	0.5-, 1-, 2-mg tabs 2 mg/mL, 4 mg/mL parenteral	2-6
clonazepam (Klonopin®)	0.5-, 1-, 2-mg tabs	0.5-6
chlordiazepoxide (Librium®)	5, 10-, 25-mg tabs 5-, 10-, 25-mg caps 100 mg parenteral	15-100
diazepam (Valium®)	2-, 5-, 10-mg tabs 15-mg caps 5 mg/mL parenteral 5 mg/5 mL, 5 mg/mL solution	2-60

Other routes of administration also can be used with some benzodiazepines (Table 9). Except for lorazepam, ox-azepam (Serax®), and temazepam (Restoril®), which are metabolized renally, other benzodiazepines are metabolized hepatically. This is important for hepatically or renally compromised patients.

Dosage: Low doses, such as the equivalent of 0.5 mg/d of clonazepam (Klonopin®), should be initially introduced to avoid sedation (Table 10). The dose should be slowly titrated up. The usual adult dosage range is equivalent to 0.5 to 6 mg/d of clonazepam. Longer-acting benzodiazepines, such as diazepam (Valium®), take up to a week to reach steady state after a dose increase, whereas shorter-acting medications, such as lorazepam, can be titrated up more rapidly, for example, every 2 to 3 days. Frequent (b.i.d. or t.i.d.) dosing for the shorter-acting benzodiazepines often is necessary to avoid interdose fluctuation of plasma levels, which can induce rebound anxiety or withdrawal symptoms. If no therapeutic effect occurs or if side effects are intolerable, an alternative benzodiazepine or a different class of medications usually should be used.

Overdose: Overdose with benzodiazepines alone usually is not fatal. However, when overdose occurs with concurrent drug use, such as with alcohol, barbiturates, antipsychotics, or antidepressants, the rate of morbidity and mortality rises significantly, with increased risks for respiratory depression, coma, seizures, and death. Benzodiazepine overdoses can be managed medically with the benzodiazepine receptor antagonist flumazenil (Romazicon®). Flumazenil is not effective in reversing the effects of opioids and opiates, or the effects of other central nervous system (CNS) depressants, even if they act partially on the GABA-A receptor, such as do alcohol and barbiturates. Flumazenil is usually administered intravenously, and has a half-life of 7 to 15 minutes, with complete elimination usually after 72 hours. The drug is hepatically cleared. The initial dose of 0.2 mg (2 mL) is administered intravenously over 30 seconds, with a repeat dose of 0.2 mg after 30 seconds. Thereafter, 0.5 mg over 30 seconds can be administered every minute, to a cumulative dose of 1 to 3 mg. Side effects include nausea, vomiting, dizziness, agitation, headache, and impaired vision.

Drug Interaction: Antacids decrease absorption of benzodiazepines. Benzodiazepines also act in concert with other CNS depressants, such as alcohol, antihistamines, barbiturates, and cyclic antidepressants, to produce sedation. All benzodiazepines, except those that do not undergo hepatic metabolism (ie, lorazepam, oxazepam, and temazepam), are increased by concomitant use with other hepatically metabolized medications, such as disulfiram (Antabuse®), cimetidine, erythromycin, estrogens (such as Premarin®), isoniazid, and serotonergic reuptake inhibitors. Anticonvulsants and smoking tend to decrease benzodiazepine levels. In addition, phenytoin (Dilantin®) and digoxin (Lanoxin®) levels may be increased by concurrent benzodiazepine use.

Discontinuation of Therapy: Because most patients on long-term benzodiazepine therapy develop dependence and would experience withdrawal symptoms on discontinuation, the drug must be tapered slowly, by about 25% a week. Benzodiazepine withdrawal syndrome includes anxiety, nervousness, diaphoresis, restlessness, irritability, fatigue, lightheadedness, tremor, insomnia, and weakness. Seizures can occur if high doses of benzodiazepines are abruptly discontinued.

Adverse Effects: Side effects include sedation and impairment of performance, such as in memory, motor coordination, and cognition. Acute doses of benzodiazepines can also produce anterograde amnesia, especially with concomitant use of alcohol. Disinhibition behavior, such as rage outbursts, aggression, increased impulsivity, and euphoria, also can occur, especially in already medically compromised patients and patients with personality disorders with a history of dyscontrol. Depressive symptoms may emerge with benzodiazepines, and usually are effectively treated with antidepressants. Allergic reactions are rare. Hepatically compromised and elderly patients are particularly at risk for adverse effects. In addition, respiration can be impaired with at-risk patients, such as those with chronic obstructive pulmonary disease (COPD). Some data indicate that benzodiazepines are teratogenic and, therefore, should not be used in pregnancy. The medication also is secreted in breast milk; therefore, breast-feeding is discouraged.

Barbiturates

Since the introduction of benzodiazepines, their advantages over barbiturates have been overt, such as safety in overdose and lesser abuse potential. Therefore, barbiturates such as secobarbital (Seconal®), pentobarbital (Nembutal®), and meprobamate (Equanil®, Miltown®) are no longer used to treat anxiety.

Buspirone

Buspirone (BuSpar®) acts on the serotonergic system as a serotonin (5-HT) agonist, decreasing serotonin turnover. It has no cross-reactivity with benzodiazepines. Buspirone has been approved for the treatment of generalized anxiety disorder, but is also often used as an augmentation agent to other medications, such as SSRIs. The chief drawback of buspirone is its slow onset of anxiolytic action, usually 1 to 2 weeks. Maximum effects occur in 4 to 6 weeks. It is metabolized hepatically, and its half-life is 2 to 11 hours. Initial dosage is 5 mg t.i.d. Doses of about 10 mg t.i.d. are effective, and it can be taken in doses up to 20 mg t.i.d. Side effects include restlessness and, less commonly, headache, GI upset, and dizziness. Its advantages are lack of sedation and little probability of abuse or withdrawal, compared with benzodiazepines.

Other Biologic Forms of Treatment

Other forms of biologic therapies are available for depressive disorders and certain anxiety disorders.

Electroconvulsive Therapy

Electroconvulsive therapy (ECT) is a safe and effective treatment for patients with major depressive disorders, especially with melancholic or psychotic features, mania, catatonia, and perhaps other forms of psychoses. It is especially useful for the treatment of populations for whom medications are contraindicated, such as pregnant women and a subpopulation of geriatric patients.

ECT involves the induction of a generalized seizure, which triggers changes in every neurotransmitter system. Successive ECT treatments downregulate beta-adrenergic receptors, which is associated with antidepressant response.

Pretreatment medical clearance is necessary. Evaluation includes standard physical, neurologic, and preanesthesia examinations. Laboratory tests include blood and urine chemistries, a chest x-ray, and an electrocardiogram. A spine x-ray is indicated if evidence suggests spinal disease. Structural brain imaging, such as computed tomography (CT) or magnetic resonance imaging (MRI), should be performed if there is evidence of seizures or a space-occupying lesion. The patient's medications should be evaluated for possible interaction with the inducted seizure and with other anesthetic medications administered during the procedure. Medications such as lithium, benzodiazepines, and clozapine (Clozaril®) should not be taken before ECT because they interfere with the seizure's threshold and duration, as do lidocaine (Xylocaine®) and theophylline.

ECT treatments are usually administered 2 to 3 times a week. Memory impairment is less common with the less frequent schedule. The number of treatments should be governed by the patient's response, and can range from 6 to 12, although as many as 20 are possible. Therapy is usually stopped if symptoms do not improve after two sessions. Induced seizures can be bilateral or unilateral. Unilateral treatments cause less memory impairment, but bilateral treatments are more potent in reducing symptoms. The patient's cognitive status should be monitored between sessions, for example, with the Mini-Mental Status Examination, to ensure that the patient regains sufficient cognitive function before the next session. If a course of treatment is successful, the patient can be started on pharmacologic maintenance therapy, or opt to have maintenance ECT to sustain remission of symptoms.

The only absolute contraindications to ECT are space-occupying brain lesions and raised intracranial pressure, which can result in brain herniation and hemorrhage. Myocardial infarction within the last 2 weeks also significantly raises the morbidity and mortality associated with ECT. The mortality rate with ECT is about 0.002%, and usually involves patients with a history of cardiac disease.

Common side effects associated with ECT are confusion and delirium. The greatest concern, however, is memory impairment. Nevertheless, data show that most patients regain baseline function 6 months after ECT treatments. Patients who do have persistent problems usually have no recall of events occurring around the treatments.

Light Therapy

The chief indication for light therapy is seasonal affective disorder, usually depressive episodes during the fall and winter. The patient is exposed to an artificial light source of about 2,500 lux (200 times brighter than indoor lighting) once to twice daily. The most common side effects are headache, eyestrain, and irritability.

Psychosurgery

Psychosurgery is usually indicated in treatment-refractory cases of depressive and anxiety disorders, especially major depressive disorder and obsessive-compulsive disorder. Patients usually would have failed multiple standard treatments before being considered for neurosurgical treatment. Selection criteria are usually stringent, but 30% to 60% of those who meet criteria for surgery can expect symptom improvement. Less than 3% become worse, and the balance remain unchanged. Modern techniques have become less invasive and more region-specific, resulting in decreased risk for cognitive and personality changes and for morbidity and mortality.

Selected Readings

American Psychiatric Association: *Diagnostic and Statistical Manual of Mental Disorders*, 4th ed. Washington, DC, American Psychiatric Association, 1994.

American Psychiatric Association: The practice of electroconvulsive therapy: recommendations for treatment, training, and privileging. A task force report of the American Psychiatric Association. Washington, DC, American Psychiatric Association, 1990.

Anafranil (clomipramine) product monograph. Basel Pharmaceuticals.

Ativan (lorazepam) product monograph. Wyeth-Ayerst Laboratories.

Blehar MC, Rosenthal NE: Seasonal affective disorders and phototherapy. Report of a National Institute of Mental Health-sponsored workshop. *Arch Gen Psychiatry* 1989;46:469-474.

Bloom FE, Kupfer DJ, eds: *Psychopharmacology: The Fourth Generation of Progress.* New York, Raven Press, 1995.

Bremner JD: A double-blind comparison of Org 3770, amitriptyline, and placebo in major depression. *J Clin Psychiatry* 1995; 56:519-525.

BuSpar (buspirone) product monograph. Bristol-Myers Squibb Company.

Cassano GB, Musetti L, Soriani A, et al: The pharmacologic treatment of depression: drug selection criteria. *Pharmacopsychiatry* 1993;26:17-23.

Celexa (citalopram) product monograph. Forrest Pharmaceuticals.

Corkin S, Twitchell TE, Sullivan EV: Modern concepts in psychiatric surgery. In: Hitchcock ER, Ballantine HT, Myerson BA, eds. Amsterdam, Netherlands, Elsevier Science Publications, 1979.

Dilsaver SC, Greden JF: Antidepressant withdrawal phenomena. *Biol Psychiatry* 1984;19:237-256.

Dilsaver SC, Greden JF, Snider RM: Antidepressant withdrawal syndromes: phenomenology and pathophysiology. *Int Clin Psychopharmacol* 1987;2:1-19.

de Boer T, Ruigt GS: The selective alpha$_2$-adrenoreceptor antagonist mirtazapine (Org 3770) enhances nonadrenergic and 5-HT$_{1A}$-mediated serotonergic neurotransmission. *CNS Drugs* 1995; 4:29-38.

de Boer T: The pharmacologic profile of mirtazapine. *J Clin Psychiatry* 1996;57:19-25.

Desyrel (trazodone) product monograph. Bristol-Myers Squibb Company.

DeVane CL, Ware MR, Lydiard RB: Pharmacokinetics, pharmacodynamics, and treatment issues of benzodiazepines: alprazolam, adinazolam, and clonazepam. *Psychopharmacol Bull* 1991;27: 463-473.

Effexor (venlafaxine) product monograph. Wyeth-Ayerst Laboratories.

Elavil (amitriptyline) product monograph. Stuart Pharmaceuticals.

Ereshefsky L: Drug interactions of antidepressants. *Psychiatr Ann* 1996;26:342-350.

Gabbard GO, ed: *Treatment of Psychiatric Disorders*. Washington, DC, American Psychiatric Press, 1995.

Hollander E, Daphne S, Gorman JM: Anxiety disorders. In: Hales RE, Yudofsky SC, Talbott JA, eds. *The American Psychiatric Press Textbook of Psychiatry*, 2nd ed. Washington, DC, American Psychiatric Press, 1994.

Hyman SE, Nestler EJ: *The Molecular Foundations of Psychiatry*. Washington, DC, American Psychiatric Association, 1993.

Jefferson JW, Greist JH: Mood disorders. In: Hales RE, Yudofsky SC, Talbott JA, eds. *The American Psychiatric Press Textbook of Psychiatry*, 2nd ed. Washington, DC, American Psychiatric Press, 1994.

Johnston JA, Lineberry CG, Ascher JA, et al: A 102-center prospective study of seizure in association with bupropion. *J Clin Psychiatry* 1991;52:450-456.

Klonopin (clonazepam) product monograph. Roche Laboratories.

Krishna KR, Steffens DC, Doraiswamy PM: Psychotropic drug interactions. *Prim Psychiatry* 1996;3:21-45.

Lam RW, Terman M, Wirz-Justice A: Light therapy for depressive disorders: indications and efficacy. *Mod Probl Pharmacopsychiatry* 1997;25:215-234.

Luvox (fluvoxamine) product monograph. Solvay Pharmaceuticals.

Marshall JB, Forker AD: Cardiovascular effects of tricyclic anti-depressant drugs: therapeutic usage, overdose, and management of complications. *Am Heart J* 1982;103:401-414.

Mindus P: Capsulotomy in anxiety disorders: a multidisciplinary study. Department of Psychiatry and Psychology, and the Department of Neurosurgery, Karolinska Hospital and Institute, Stockholm, Sweden, 1991.

Nardil (phenelzine) product monograph. Parke-Davis.

Norpramin (desipramine) product monograph. Hoechst Marion Roussel.

Pamelor (nortriptyline) product monograph. Sandoz Pharmaceuticals.

Parnate (tranylcypromine) product monograph. SmithKline Beecham Pharmaceuticals.

Patris M, Bouchard JM, Bougerol T, et al: Citalopram versus fluoxetine: a double-blind, controlled, multicentre, phase III trial in patients with unipolar major depression treated in general practice. *Int Clin Psychopharmacol* 1996;11:129-136.

Paxil (paroxetine) product monograph. SmithKline Beecham Pharmaceuticals.

Prozac (fluoxetine) product monograph. Eli Lilly and Company.

Rabheru K, Persad E: A review of continuation and maintenance electroconvulsive therapy. *Can J Psychiatry* 1997;42:476-484.

Remeron (mirtazapine) product monograph. Organon, Inc.

Roy-Byrne PP, Dager SR, Cowley DS, et al: Relapse and rebound following discontinuation of benzodiazepine treatment of panic attacks: alprazolam versus diazepam. *Am J Psychiatry* 1989;146:860-865.

Serzone (nefazodone) product monograph. Bristol-Myers Squibb Company.

Shader RI, von Moltke LL, Schmider J, et al: The clinician and drug interactions—an update. *J Clin Psychopharmacol* 1996;16:197-201.

Silver JM, Yudofsky SC, Hurowitz GI: Psychopharmacology and electroconvulsive therapy. In: Hales RE, Yudofsky SC, Talbott JA, eds. *The American Psychiatric Press Textbook of Psychiatry,* 2nd ed. Washington, DC, American Psychiatric Press, 1994.

Stoudemire A, Fogel BS: *Medical Psychiatric Practice*, Vol 3. Washington, DC, American Psychiatric Press, 1995.

Tofranil (imipramine) product monograph. Geigy Pharmaceuticals.

Wellbutrin and Zyban (bupropion) product monographs. Glaxo Wellcome Company.

Xanax (alprazolam) product monograph. Upjohn Pharmaceuticals.

Zajecka J, Tracy KA, Mitchell S: Discontinuation symptoms after treatment with serotonin reuptake inhibitors: a literature review. *J Clin Psychiatry* 1997;58:291-297.

Zoloft (sertraline) product monograph. Roerig division, Pfizer Inc.

Section II: Depression: Diagnosis and Management

Chapter 3

Depression: Overview and Diagnosis

D epression is both a symptom as well as a syndrome or disorder. It exacts economic as well as quality-of-life tolls on the individual and society. The National Institute of Mental Health has estimated the annual direct cost of depression at $12.4 billion. Indirect costs, which include time lost from work, are estimated at $30 billion. These figures do not account for the additional cost of human suffering, however. Suicide in patients with major depression accounts for 12,000 deaths each year, many of them in the elderly. Other consequences of depression are social deprivation, loneliness, poor quality of life, increased use of health and home-care services, cognitive decline in the elderly, impairment of activities of daily living, and increased nonsuicide mortality.

The differential diagnoses are vast, and treatment implications vary according to the type of depression and associated comorbid conditions. An organic etiology for the depression must first be ruled out, especially for those patients who first present with this symptom, and for those with comorbid conditions.

The complaint of depression often refers to a subjective pervasive feeling of being 'down' or 'blue,' or a loss of interest or pleasure (anhedonia). However, many people with depression do not describe themselves as feeling subjectively depressed, especially in mentally retarded, child/

adolescent, and geriatric populations. These individuals may present with irritability, or are observed by others to seem depressed or uninterested in life. Examples include appearing tearful or sad, or not taking part in normally pleasurable activities. However, other symptoms often accompany a depressed mood or anhedonia, and the patient may present with these complaints on initial evaluation. Disturbances in sleep and appetite, either excessive or diminished, are common. A weight change of more than 5% over a month may accompany these symptoms. Patients with clinical depression also may complain of a loss of energy or feeling fatigued nearly every day, a decrease in concentration, or decreased ability to make decisions. Patients may be tense or agitated or, conversely, have slowed motor function. Many patients also experience a sense of diminished self-worth or excessive guilt, and tend to ruminate about things. This is not merely self-reproach. In addition, patients with comorbid conditions who take concomitant medications also can have symptoms that can appear similar to depressive symptoms (eg, insomnia, weight loss, fatigue), which can complicate the picture.

Most importantly, the clinician must determine if a patient has recurrent thoughts of death (not merely a fear of dying), whether the individual has passive suicidal ideation (ie, suicidal thoughts without a specific plan, or would rather be dead than alive), or whether the patient has active suicidal ideation (ie, a specific plan for suicide, or has actually attempted to take his or her own life). The most dangerous time for suicidal patients is when they start feeling more energized but still have thoughts of killing themselves. This period is most common during initial treatment, and soon after discharge for hospitalized patients. Approximately 50% of people who commit suicide have a primary diagnosis of depression. Early increased risk factors in depressed patients are the presence of panic attacks, psychic anxiety, anhedonia, substance abuse, and prominent insomnia. Long-term risk factors include hopelessness, suicidal ideation, and prior suicide attempts.

Case Report

PN, a 36-year-old, separated, white male and an unemployed stock market expert, presented with a 3-year history of feeling depressed and down, and complained of not finding anything enjoyable anymore. He had lost his high-paying job, and he and his wife were getting a divorce because he had not been able to 'function like I used to.' He also reported that he had gained considerable weight associated with an increased appetite, slept a lot, stayed in bed for long periods, felt tired and run down all the time, and seemed to move in slow motion. He was unable to concentrate as he had previously been able, such as reading, and had a short attention span and significant irritability. He spent a lot of time ruminating about how he had had the 'perfect life' and how awful everything had become. He also often thought that being dead would be an 'easy out' because he would no longer have to suffer such agony, but he had never had a plan to commit suicide nor had he attempted suicide. He claimed he could never kill himself because of his children, and because, "I don't have much energy to do anything right now anyway." He felt that his life was doomed and that he would never get any better.

On mental status examination, the patient was restless and fidgety, shaking his legs almost constantly. His eye contact was poor and he slumped over in his chair. He appeared to be disheveled. His speech was low and monotonous, with a latency between his physician's questions and his answers. He described his mood as 'depressed' and 'anxious' and his affect was anxious and dysphoric. He had passive suicidal ideation, but denied any active suicidal ideation, paranoia, homicidal intent, hallucinations, or delusions. He had reasonable insight into his problems and demonstrated intact judgment by seeking medical treatment. He was alert and oriented with no apparent cognitive deficits.

This patient was suffering from a major depression with significant anxiety symptoms. Although he denied active suicidal ideation, he would be at risk for suicide because, as he responds to treatment, he would gain increasing energy and perhaps act on his impulses. He was too ill to benefit from psychotherapy, but would probably be a good candidate once stabilized on medications.

The clinician must also determine whether a patient has or has had episodes of hypomania or mania, because this has important treatment implications. Symptoms of mania include feelings of elatedness or irritability, inflated self-esteem or grandiosity, decreased need for sleep, pressure to keep talking, flight of ideas (accelerated continuous flow of ideas with abrupt changes from topic to topic), distractibility, increase in goal-directed behavior, an excessive involvement in pleasurable but risky activities for 1 week, and hypomania for 4 days. Initial treatment with an antidepressant can trigger a manic/hypomanic episode in patients with a manic-depressive tendency. Therefore, these patients must first be stabilized with a mood stabilizer such as lithium (Eskalith®, Lithonate®, Lithobid®), valproate (Depakene®), carbamazepine (Tegretol®), or gabapentin (Neurontin®), before an antidepressant is started.

The presence of concomitant psychosis should also be determined because these patients may require antipsychotic medications. Symptoms of psychosis include hallucinations (sensory perceptions, such as voices, that occur without an external stimulus, as opposed to illusions, which are perceptual misconceptions triggered by external stimuli), and delusions (fixed false beliefs that are not ordinarily accepted by the person's culture). Hallucinations may be auditory, visual, gustatory, olfactory, somatic, or tactile. Delusions include bizarre delusions, delusional jealousy, delusions of being controlled by an outside force, and erotomanic, grandiose, referential, and persecutory delusions.

Patients with depression also may present with catatonia, characterized by motor immobility (catalepsy) or stupor, excessive motor activity that usually is purposeless and not in response to external stimuli, negativism or mutism, peculiarities of voluntary movement (eg, assuming bizarre poses [posturing], stereotypy, prominent mannerisms or grimacing), and echolalia (repeating what someone else has just said) or echopraxia (repeatedly imitating another's movements). During severe catatonia, close supervision is important to avoid self-injurious behavior or harm to others. Other consequences of catatonia include exhaustion, malnutrition, and hyperpyrexia.

Depression can have different subtypes. Depression with melancholic features refers to a distinct depression that does not improve even temporarily (lack of mood reactivity), is worse in the morning (diurnal variation), and includes early morning awakening, motor retardation or agitation, significant weight loss or anorexia, and excessive or inappropriate guilt. Individuals with melancholic depression are less likely to have a premorbid personality disorder, or to have a clear stressor/precipitant to the depression. Melancholic depression equally affects both genders, is usually more severe, and occurs more commonly in older individuals.

Atypical depression is characterized by mood reactivity (mood brightens in response to actually or potentially positive events), significant weight gain or increase in appetite, increased sleep, heavy feelings in the arms and legs (leaden paralysis), and a long-standing pattern of interpersonal rejection sensitivity that results in significant functional impairment. Personality disorders and anxiety disorders are more common in patients with atypical depression. Depression with atypical features is more common in women, in those with earlier age of onset, and in those who have a more chronic course of illness.

Depression also can present during the first 4 weeks of the postpartum period in some women. A fluctuating course and mood lability tend to be more common in postpartum depression. Suicidal ideation, obsessional thoughts of violence to the newborn, lack of concentration, and motor agitation may be present. Psychotic symptoms may be present as well, including delusions about the infant. In addition, extreme anxiety, panic attacks, spontaneous crying after the usual duration of 'baby blues' (3 to 7 days postpartum), lack of interest in the infant, and difficulty falling asleep may also occur.

Depression may have a seasonal pattern. Episodes usually begin in fall or winter and remit in spring. Symptoms of seasonal depression include prominent lack of energy, increased sleep, overeating and weight gain, and carbohydrate cravings. Younger individuals tend to be at higher risk for winter depression, with increased incidence in females.

Subtypes of depression addressed in the following chapters include major depression, bipolar disorder, cyclothymia, chronic depression, bereavement, adjustment disorder, depression and special populations (eg, the elderly, pregnancy, general medical conditions such as cerebrovascular accidents, myocardial infarction, and HIV infection), and refractory depression. Diagnostic criteria, differential diagnosis, and treatment options for each type of depression are addressed.

Selected Readings

American Psychiatric Association: *Diagnostic and Statistical Manual of Mental Disorders*, 4th ed. Washington, DC, American Psychiatric Association, 1994.

Barklage NE: Evaluation and management of the suicidal patient. *Emerg Care Q* 1991;7:9-17.

Bostic JQ, Wilens T, Spencer T, et al: Juvenile mood disorders and office psychopharmacology. *Pediatr Clin North Am* 1997; 44:1487-1503.

Cohen LJ: Rational drug use in the treatment of depression. *Pharmacotherapy* 1997;17:45-61.

Emmett KR: Nonspecific and atypical presentation of disease in the older patient. *Geriatrics* 1998;53:50-52.

Faedda GL, Tondo L, Teicher MH, et al: Seasonal mood disorders. Patterns of seasonal recurrence in mania and depression. *Arch Gen Psychiatry* 1993;50:17-23.

Fava M, Uebelacker LA, Alpert JE, et al: Major depressive subtypes and treatment response. *Biol Psychiatry* 1997;42:568-576.

Fawcett J, Scheftner WA, Fogg L, et al: Time-related predictors of suicide in major affective disorder. *Am J Psychiatry* 1990;147: 1189-1194.

Goodwin FK, Jamison KR: *Manic-Depressive Illness*. New York, Oxford University Press, 1990.

Greist JH, Jefferson JW: *Depression and Its Treatment*, revised ed. Washington, DC, American Psychiatric Press, 1992.

Hopkins J, Marcus M, Campbell SB: Postpartum depression: a critical review. *Psychol Bull* 1984;95:498-515.

Jefferson JW, Greist JH: Mood disorders. In: Hales RE, Yudofsky SC, Talbott JA, eds. *The American Psychiatric Press Textbook of Psychiatry*, 2nd ed. Washington, DC, American Psychiatric Press, 1994.

Llewellyn AM, Stowe ZN, Nemeroff CB: Depression during pregnancy and the puerperium. *J Clin Psychiatry* 1997;58:26-32.

Nelson JC, Mazure CM, Jatlow PI: Does melancholia predict response in major depression? *J Affect Disord* 1990;18:157-165.

Palsson S, Skoog I: The epidemiology of affective disorders in the elderly: a review. *Int Clin Psychopharmacol* 1997;12:S3-S13.

Pfuhlmann B, Stober G: The importance of a differentiated psychopathology of catatonia. *Acta Psychiatr Scand* 1997;95:357-359.

Physicians' Desk Reference, 51st ed. Medical Economics Data Production Co, Montvale, NJ, 1997.

Robertson HA, Lam RW, Stewart JN, et al: Atypical depressive symptoms and clusters in unipolar and bipolar depression. *Acta Psychiatr Scand* 1996;94:421-427.

Stowe ZN, Nemeroff CB: Women at risk for postpartum-onset major depression. *Am J Obstet Gynecol* 1995;173:639-645.

Chapter 4

Major Depressive Disorder

Major depression affects a large percentage of the population. The lifetime prevalence rate is 10% to 25% for women, and 5% to 12% for men. These prevalence rates are unrelated to ethnicity, education, income, or marital status. Major depression has a high mortality rate: up to 15% of patients commit suicide. Moreover, for patients 55 years of age and older, the suicide rate is four times the death rate of the overall population. Patients with major depression report more pain and physical illness, make more visits to doctors, and have decreased overall functioning.

The diagnostic criteria for major depressive disorder, according to DSM-IV, are the presence of one or more major depressive episodes in the absence of mania or hypomania. A major depressive episode is defined as 5 or more symptoms for at least 2 weeks occurring nearly every day for most of the day, representing a change from baseline functioning, plus at least either depressed mood or anhedonia. Table 1 lists these symptoms. Five or more symptoms must be present, and the episode can not be attributable to bereavement after the loss of a loved one, to the effects of drugs or medications, or to a physical condition such as hypothyroidism.

Comorbid psychiatric illnesses include the presence of dysthymia in 10% to 25% of patients with major depression ('double depression'), anxiety disorders (eg, panic disorder, obsessive-compulsive disorder), eating disorders

Table 1: Symptoms of Major Depressive Episode

- Depressed mood
- Marked decreased interest or pleasure in activities (anhedonia)
- Significant weight change or change in appetite
- Insomnia or hypersomnia
- Psychomotor agitation or retardation
- Loss of energy or fatigue
- Feelings of worthlessness or excessive/inappropriate guilt
- Decreased concentration
- Recurrent thoughts of death, or suicidal ideation with or without a plan

(eg, anorexia nervosa, bulimia), personality disorders (eg, borderline personality disorder), and substance abuse disorders. Up to 25% of patients with certain chronic medical conditions also develop major depression; these include diabetes, myocardial infarction, stroke, and carcinoma.

Major depression can arise at any age, but the average age of onset is in the mid 20s. The course for recurrent major depression is variable; some patients have isolated episodes separated by years, others experience clusters of episodes, and still others have a progressively increasing number of episodes with age. About half of patients with one major depressive episode have a second, and individuals who have had two episodes have a 70% chance of having a third. In addition, 5% to 10% of patients with a major depressive episode subsequently develop a manic episode (eg, bipolar or manic-depressive disorder). Symptoms of a major depressive episode

Table 2: Differential Diagnoses of Major Depressive Disorder

- Mood disorder from a general medical condition

- Substance-induced mood disorder

- Dementia in the elderly

- Psychotic disorder with depressive symptoms (eg, postpsychotic depression in schizophrenia or schizoaffective disorder)

- Dysthymia, which has fewer symptoms than major depressive disorder, but lasts for at least 2 years in adults and 1 year in adolescents and children

- Bipolar disorder with mixed manic episodes or mania with significant irritability

- Adjustment disorder with depressed mood, which occurs after a significant stressor and does not meet full criteria for a major depressive episode

- Bereavement, which has symptoms similar to a major depressive episode but lasts less than 2 months, and without concomitant psychosis (other than the patient hearing the voice of or seeing the image of the deceased) or significant suicidality that is not confined to the feelings of a survivor

can develop over days or weeks, with a prodrome that may include anxiety and mild depressive symptoms lasting up to weeks or months. An untreated episode usually lasts 6 months or longer, regardless of age of onset. In most cases, patients have a complete remission. In 20% to 30% of cases, remission is only partial; and in 5% to 10% of the cases, the major depressive episode can continue for 2 or more years. The differential diagnoses of major depressive disorder are listed in Table 2.

Treatment

This chapter concentrates more on biologic interventions rather than on psychotherapeutic modalities, although if an individual is able to participate in psychotherapy, a combination of medication and psychotherapy yields the best response rate. Shorter-term psychotherapeutic interventions, such as cognitive and interpersonal therapies, have been shown to be as useful as pharmacologic approaches for the milder forms of depression. However, the more severe depressions tend to respond better to pharmacotherapy or electroconvulsive therapy (ECT).

Between 60% and 80% of patients with major depression respond to a single trial of medication with an adequately high dose over 6 weeks. Of the remainder, most will have at least a partial response. Between 10% and 15% of patients do not substantially improve. For those who do not fully respond to the first medication trial, a combination of medications or a switch to a different medication often is most beneficial. Most patients who are refractory to medication treatment often respond to ECT. However, many patients who are termed treatment refractory often have not received adequate trials of medication in dose or duration. In addition, patients with comorbid psychiatric disorders, such as personality or psychotic disorders, have a lower response rate.

For major depression with psychotic features, most patients respond best to ECT or to a combination of an antidepressant and an antipsychotic (70% to 80%), compared with 30% to 50% response rates when treated with either alone. Atypical depression (characterized by reversed vegetative symptoms such as increased sleep and appetite, rejection sensitivity, prominent anxiety) tends to respond better to monoamine oxidase inhibitors (MAOIs) or selective serotonin reuptake inhibitors (SSRIs)

Table 3: Factors in Choosing an Antidepressant for Outpatients

- Past response
- Response of a family member; a favorable response in a family member often suggests a favorable response in the patient
- Depressive subtype
- Comorbid condition(s)
- Medication side effect profile; certain side effects may decrease compliance
- Adverse medication interactions
- Cost

---

than to tricyclic antidepressants (TCAs). The more severe depressions in inpatient populations tend to respond better to tricyclics or agents that affect both serotonin and norepinephrine (eg, venlafaxine [Effexor®]) rather than to SSRIs. In general outpatient populations, no class of antidepressant has any efficacy advantages. Table 3 lists factors to consider in the choice of antidepressant.

Most older medications, such as the MAOIs and TCAs, have a less favorable side effect profile than do the newer medications, such as the SSRIs, serotonin-norepinephrine reuptake inhibitors (SNRIs), and atypical antidepressants. Therefore, MAOIs and TCAs must be started at lower doses and titrated up to the target range. On the other hand, many SSRIs and SNRIs can be started at an effective dose. Blood levels for some antidepressants can be measured to check compliance and to evaluate toxicity and side effects. However, blood levels for only a few antidepressants (eg, nortriptyline [Pamelor®], imipramine [Tofranil®], and desipramine [Norpramin®]) correlate with therapeutic response.

Most antidepressant medication effects evolve slowly over many days or weeks. An adequate trial involves an appropriate dose for at least 4 to 6 weeks. If response is inadequate, changing to a different antidepressant (after a washout period if necessary), or augmenting the antidepressant with another agent such as a mood stabilizer (eg, lithium [Eskalith®, Lithobid®, Lithonate®]), thyroid hormone (eg, liothyronine [Cytomel®]), another antidepressant (eg, combining an SSRI with a noradrenergic or dopamine reuptake inhibitor), or buspirone (BuSpar®, a 5-HT_{1A} agonist), may be effective. Patients who still do not respond should be reevaluated for the primary diagnosis or the presence of comorbid disorders, which may complicate treatment outcome. Treatment-refractory depression is addressed further in Chapter 8.

Once the patient has achieved full remission, maintenance treatment is recommended for at least another 6 months to reduce the rate of relapse. However, because of the recurrent nature of major depression, preventive (long-term) therapy often is indicated, especially for patients with more than two prior depressive episodes. In addition, full-dose maintenance treatments (eg, the same dose required to remit an acute episode) have been found to be more protective against recurrences in many cases, as opposed to lower-dose treatments.

Selected Readings

American Psychiatric Association: *Diagnostic and Statistical Manual of Mental Disorders*, 4th ed. Washington, DC, American Psychiatric Press, 1994.

American Psychiatric Association: Practice guidelines for major depressive disorder in adults. *Am J Psychiatry* 1993;150:1-26.

American Psychiatric Association: Task Force on the Use of Laboratory Tests in Psychiatry. Tricyclic antidepressants—blood level measurements and clinical outcome: an APA Task Force report. *Am J Psychiatry* 1985;142:155-162.

Cohen LJ: Rational drug use in the treatment of depression. *Pharmacotherapy* 1997;17:45-61.

Elkin I, Shea MT, Watkins JT, et al: National Institute of Mental Health Treatment of Depression Collaborative Research Program. General effectiveness of treatments. *Arch Gen Psychiatry* 1989; 46:971-982.

Jefferson JW, Greist JH: Mood disorders. In: Hales RE, Yudofsky SC, Talbott JA, eds. *The American Psychiatric Press Textbook of Psychiatry*, 2nd ed. Washington, DC, American Psychiatric Press, 1994.

Keller MB, Klerman GL, Lavori PW, et al: Long-term outcome of episodes of major depression. Clinical and public health significance. *JAMA* 1984;252:788-792.

Keller MB, Shapiro RW: "Double depression": superimposition of acute depressive episodes on chronic depressive disorders. *Am J Psychiatry* 1982;139:438-442.

Klerman GL, Weissman MM, Rounsaville BJ, et al: *Interpersonal Psychotherapy of Depression*. New York, Basic Books, 1984.

Kupfer DJ: Long-term treatment of depression. *J Clin Psychiatry* 1991;52:28-34.

Regier DA, Burke JD Jr, Burke KC: Comorbidity of affective and anxiety disorders in the NIMH Epidemiologic Catchment Area Program. In: Maser JD, Cloninger CR, eds. *Comorbidity of Mood and Anxiety Disorders*. Washington, DC, American Psychiatric Press, 1990.

Thase ME: Relapse and recurrence in unipolar major depression: short-term and long-term approaches. *J Clin Psychiatry* 1990; 51:51-57.

Weissman MM, Leaf PJ, Tischler GL, et al: Affective disorders in five United States communities. *Psychol Med* 1988;18:141-153.

Chapter **5**

Bipolar Disorder and Cyclothymia

Bipolar disorder is defined as the presence of one or more manic (in the case of bipolar I disorder) or hypomanic (in the case of bipolar II disorder) episodes, with or without major depressive episodes. In other words, unipolar mania consists of mania only without any major depression, bipolar I disorder consists of mania with major depression, and bipolar II disorder consists of hypomania and major depression. However, the incidence of unipolar mania is very low. The morbidity and mortality associated with bipolar disorder are significant. The Medical Practice Information Demonstration Project (1979) estimated that an untreated woman with onset of bipolar disorder at age 25 would lose 9.2 years of life and 14.2 years of major life activity.

The lifetime prevalence of bipolar I disorder is 1.2%, and 0.5% for bipolar II disorder. Bipolar I disorder represents about 20% of all major mood disorders. The age of onset for bipolar disorder peaks at 18 years in men and 20 years in women. Mania first appearing in the elderly is not rare, but is generally associated with an organic etiology. Bipolar disorder has no gender preponderance, except in the case of rapid cyclers (4 or more manic/hypomanic episodes a year), in whom women tend to be overrepresented.

Ten percent to 15% of bipolar patients commit suicide. Violence, such as spousal and child abuse, often occurs

> ## Table 1: Differential Diagnoses of Bipolar Disorder
>
> - Mood disorder from a general medical condition
> - Substance-induced mood disorder
> - Major depressive disorder and dysthymia
> - Psychotic disorders (eg, schizoaffective disorder, schizophrenia, delusional disorder)
> - Cyclothymia

during manic/hypomanic episodes. Other associated problems include school truancy and failure, and antisocial behavior. Associated mental disorders include eating disorders, attention-deficit hyperactivity disorder, anxiety disorders, and substance-related disorders.

Case Report

MM was a 24-year-old, single, white female undergraduate with a family history of bipolar disorder. She had her first depressive episode at about age 18 but was never treated for it. She had her first manic episode at about age 20. During that manic episode, she was also psychotic and paranoid, and required an inpatient admission. After being stabilized on lithium (Lithobid®), she returned to college, managed to maintain her A average, and joined the college council. She was feeling much better, but had gained weight and developed acne from the medication she was taking, so she stopped taking it. Several weeks later, her friends noticed that she was not herself, was erratic and unpredictable, and would go for long walks in the middle of the night. Then she started accusing her boyfriend of belonging to the FBI and spying on her. This resulted in a second admission, during which she was restabilized on medication. She was discharged, but then developed a depression, which resulted in her losing an entire semester. She continued to take her medications, but a year later developed mania and psychosis again. This time she was switched to a different regimen of valproate (Depakote®), to which she did not respond, then to carbamazepine (Tegretol®). She started to improve, but then had multiple relapses of both mania and depression, with closer and closer cycles, and required alterations in treatment plans and medication regimens. She was finally stabilized on a combination of lithium and carbamazepine with fair control of her symptoms. Unfortunately, she dropped out of college and returned to live with her parents. However, she planned to enter a day treatment program and ultimately return to school and get her degree.

Bipolar disorder is recurrent. More than 90% of individuals who have a single manic episode have future episodes. Manic/hypomanic episodes usually precede or follow a depressive episode in a characteristic pattern for each individual. The interval between episodes tends to decrease with age. Most patients with bipolar disorder return to baseline after a manic/hypomanic episode. However, 15% to 30% of patients only have partial remission and exhibit interepisodic symptoms. Incomplete return to baseline between episodes tends to occur more commonly in patients with concomitant psychotic features during mania. Between 10% and 15% of adolescents with recurrent major depressive episodes develop bipolar disorder. Mixed episodes of coexisting manic and depressive symptoms tend to be more common in adolescents and young adults than in older adults. Women with bipolar disorder have an increased risk of developing postpartum episodes, which often are psychotic. First-degree relatives of bipolar patients have increased rates of both bipolar I and II disorders, as well as major depressive disorder. The differential diagnoses of bipolar disorder are outlined in Table 1.

Cyclothymia is a chronic, fluctuating mood disturbance involving numerous hypomanic episodes and depressive symptoms that do not meet criteria for major depressive episodes for at least 2 years, or 1 year in children and adolescents. Substance-related and sleep disorders may be associated with cyclothymia. Cyclothymia has no gender preponderance, and it tends to have an early age of onset. It has a lifetime prevalence of up to 1%. The risk of a cyclothymic patient developing bipolar I or II disorder is 15% to 50%. Other mood disorders and substance-related disorders also carry a familial risk. In addition to substance-induced mood disorder and mood disorder from a general medical condition, differential diagnosis also includes borderline personality disorder.

Case Report

AM was a 30-year-old, married, white stockbroker who sought treatment of periodic depressions that would dampen his 'hyper personality,' which he said was essential for his line of work. He described periods of feeling slowed down and tired and not being as productive at his job as he usually was. He also would not feel like socializing and would stay at home a lot. His wife said that, during these times, he seemed to be quiet. On questioning, he reported that when he felt good, he would talk a mile a minute, juggle many different projects at the same time, and would be 'hyper and bouncing off the walls.' He made substantial sales commissions during this time and was extremely productive. 'It's like he's a different person,' according to his wife. The patient wanted to be treated for the 'down' periods but did not want to be treated for the hypomanic episodes because it 'feels too good and it makes me a lot of money.'

Treatment

Even more so than for major depressive disorder, pharmacotherapy is key to bipolar patients' treatment, recovery and long-term well-being, although psychotherapy is still an important adjunct to treatment. For severe acute manic episodes, inpatient treatment usually is necessary because these patients often require a safe environment. Mood stabilizers, such as lithium (lithium carbonate, Eskalith®, Eskalith CR®, Lithobid®, Lithonate®, Lithotabs™, lithium citrate syrup, Cibalith-S®), valproate (valproic acid, Depakene®), carbamazepine (Tegretol®), gabapentin (Neurontin®), and lamotrigine (Lamictal®) have a relatively slow onset of action (usually 10 to 14 days). Therefore, initial cotreatment with an antipsychotic or a benzodiazepine may be necessary to initially stabilize some patients. Lithium is the most studied mood stabilizer and remains the first choice of treatment in many cases. It is effective in 70% to 80% of cases. However, other mood stabilizers, such as valproate, have been shown to be just as effective, and perhaps more so in rapid cyclers and for dysphoric or mixed mania. Combined treatment with lithium and an anticonvulsant also can be used if monotherapy fails. Other agents that have been used to treat mania include calcium-channel blockers, beta-blockers, clozapine (Clozaril®), and olanzapine (Zyprexa®). Lastly, electroconvulsive therapy (ECT) also has been effective in a small number of patients, and remains viable for pregnant bipolar women.

Lithium has been shown to be helpful for acute depression in bipolar patients, with a 75% to 80% response. Antidepressants should be instituted *after* a patient has been stabilized with a mood stabilizer, because antidepressants can induce mania/hypomania and rapid cycling. Tricyclic antidepressants (TCAs) are less effective in bipolar depression than in unipolar depression, while monoamine oxidase inhibitors (MAOIs), selective serotonin reuptake inhibitors (SSRIs), serotonin-norepinephrine reuptake inhibitors (SNRIs), and other atypical antidepressants are promising. Antidepressants should be discontinued after the depressive episode remits.

Maintenance therapy usually is required in bipolar patients, because recurrence is high if treatment is discontinued (about 28 times increased risk of a bipolar episode). More disturbing, the efficacy of lithium is decreased with retreatment after discontinuation. If a patient becomes resistant to monotherapy, combination treatment with two mood stabilizers can be helpful.

Mood Stabilizers

Lithium

Lithium is available in many forms: lithium carbonate (Eskalith® 300-mg tabs/capsules, lithium carbonate 300-mg tabs/capsules, Lithonate® 300-mg capsules, Lithotabs™ 300-mg tablets); slow-release lithium carbonate (Lithobid® 300-mg tabs, Eskalith CR® 450-mg tabs); and lithium citrate syrup (Cibalith®-S 8 mEq/5 mL, which is equivalent to 300 mg lithium carbonate).

Lithium has a half-life of about 24 hours, and takes about 5 days to reach steady state. The standard forms produce peak serum levels in 1.5 to 2 hours and slow-release forms in 4 to 4.5 hours. However, the half-life can be prolonged in the elderly and the renally compromised. The carbonate and citrate forms usually are taken t.i.d., whereas the slow-release carbonate forms (Lithobid® and Eskalith CR®) require only once-a-day dosing. The sustained-release forms tend to have fewer peaks and troughs, and therefore cause less tremor and nausea, as well as less polyuria and fewer renal structural abnormalities. However, because of delayed absorption, more diarrhea may be associated with their use.

Baseline workup should include a physical examination, medical history, blood urea nitrogen (BUN) and creatinine levels, thyroid function tests (TFTs), complete blood count (CBC), and an electrocardiogram (ECG) and pregnancy tests, if appropriate. Lithium is usually started at 300 to 600 mg/d, with lower doses for the elderly or medically ill, and then titrated slowly to a target dose depending on therapeutic and side effect profiles, and blood levels. Blood levels should initially be checked every 5 days to adjust the dose. Blood levels for acute treatment of mania range from 1.0 to 1.2 mEq/L, and from 0.8 to 1.0 mEq/L for maintenance treatment. Levels above 1.5 mEq/L usually are toxic. The usual dosage range of lithium is 900 to 1,500 mg/d, although doses may reach 3,000 mg/d to achieve therapeutic levels.

Side effects of lithium tend to occur early during therapy. Gastrointestinal (GI) side effects include nausea, vomiting, and diarrhea. Lithium can also cause renal problems, such as problems with concentration of urine, polyuria, nephrogenic diabetes insipidus, some cases of nephrotic syndrome that are reversible, and edema. Neurologic symptoms include tremor, some cases of pseudotumor cerebri, neuromuscular irritability, ataxia, extrapyramidal symptoms, visual disturbances, and difficulty concentrating. Thyroid effects include hypothyroidism in about 5% of cases, and increased levels of thyroid-stimulating hormone (TSH). Cardiac effects include T-wave inversion or flattening, which is reversible and almost always benign, arrhythmias in patients with preexisting cardiac disease, and some cases of sudden death in cardiac patients. Dermatologic effects include acne and psoriasis. Hematologic effects include benign leukocytosis. Patients may also experience weight gain, which often leads to noncompliance. Calcium and parathyroid hormone may be mildly elevated.

Lithium toxicity can be precipitated by sodium-wasting diuretics, dehydration, changes in diet, nonsteroidal anti-inflammatory drugs (NSAIDs) other than aspirin, tetracycline, metronidazole (Flagyl®), angiotensin-converting enzyme (ACE) inhibitors, and renal compromise. All of these factors can raise lithium levels. Dialysis is indicated if levels are greater than 3 mEq/L, or if signs of toxicity are severe. Drugs that lower lithium levels include osmotic diuretics, acetazolamide, theophylline, and caffeine. Routine tests to monitor lithium therapy include following lithium levels, creatinine levels, and TSH every 3 to 6 months once the patient is stabilized. Follow-up ECGs also should be done as clinically indicated.

Valproate

Valproate is available in many forms: 250-mg capsules (valproic acid—Depakene®); 125-mg sprinkle capsules (Depakote® Sprinkle); 125-, 250-, and 500-mg enteric-coated tablets (Depakote®); and 250 mg/5 mL syrup (Depakene®). It has been very well studied in bipolar illness, rapid cycling, and mixed mania.

Valproate is 80% to 95% protein bound, and is metabolized by the liver. It has a short half-life, about 8 hours. Therefore, divided doses usually are recommended, but have not been found to be more effective than single dosing for bipolar disorder. Baseline blood tests should include liver function tests (LFTs) and CBC with platelets. Valproate should not be administered in patients with liver disease.

Valproate is initiated at a dose of 250 mg/d with meals, with a maximum dose of 1,800 mg/d. Antimanic drug levels may be higher than those for antiepileptic effects with regard to anticonvulsant drug use. The target blood level range for valproate is 50 to 120 µg/mL. Levels should be obtained weekly until the patient is stabilized. Follow-up tests should include valproate levels, LFTs, and a CBC every 6 months.

Side effects of valproate include GI effects such as nausea, vomiting, and diarrhea. Patients may also experience sedation, tremor, ataxia, alopecia, and weight gain, which again often leads to noncompliance. Valproate can also produce bleeding tendencies from thrombocytopenia and, less commonly, hyperammonemia. Some idiosyncratic effects include hepatitis, pancreatitis, agranulocytosis, drug rashes, and polycystic ovaries in young women. Valproate can increase levels of several drugs when taken concomitantly, including TCAs, SSRIs, phenytoin (Dilantin®), and phenobarbital. It can be displaced by other protein-bound drugs leading to increased valproate levels; these include aspirin and warfarin (Coumadin®). Valproate levels can be lowered by carbamazepine.

Carbamazepine

Carbamazepine is available in many forms: carbamazepine 100- and 200-mg tabs, Atretol 200-mg tabs, Tegretol® 100- and 200-mg tabs, and Tegretol® suspension 100 mg/5 mL. Its absorption is slow: peak serum levels are achieved in 4 to 8 hours, or later in some cases. Carbamazepine is poorly soluble in GI fluids. It is 65% to 80% protein bound, and is metabolized by the liver. The elimination half-life is 18 to 55 hours in healthy individuals; however, the half-life decreases to 5 to 20 hours with repeat dosing because of autoinduction (ie, inducing its own metabolism by the hepatic P-450 system). Autoinduction usually plateaus after 3 to 5 weeks.

Baseline work-up should include a medical history, physical examination, CBC with platelets, and liver and renal function tests. Patients with blood dyscrasias should be followed very carefully. Hepatically compromised patients should be started at half the usual dose and titrated over a longer period of time. Carbamazepine is usually initiated at 200 mg/d, and titrated to about 1,000 mg/d, with a dosage range of 200 to 1,800 mg/d. The target blood level is 8 to 12 µg/mL. Blood levels, CBC, and LFTs should be followed about every 2 weeks during the first 2 months of treatment until the patient stabilizes. Blood levels and tests then can be followed every 3 to 6 months.

Side effects include dizziness, ataxia, sedation, dysarthria, diplopia, reversible mild leukopenia, and reversible mild increase in LFTs. Less common effects include tremor, memory disturbance and confusion, cardiac conduction delays, and syndrome of inappropriate antidiuretic hormone (SIADH). Rare but serious side effects include hepatitis, exfoliative dermatitis, aplastic anemia, agranulocytosis, leukopenia, thrombocytopenia, and lenticular opacities.

Carbamazepine decreases the effects of warfarin, ethosuximide (Zarontin®), valproate, tetracycline, benzodiazepines, and TCAs. It may increase the effects of digitalis (digoxin, Lanoxin®), and has unpredictable effects on phenytoin. Erythromycin, isoniazid (INH), cimetidine (Tagamet®), and SSRIs can increase carbamazepine levels.

Gabapentin

Gabapentin is a newer anticonvulsant that has been shown to have mood-stabilizing qualities. It is available in 100-, 300-, and 400-mg capsules. It is rapidly absorbed after oral ingestion: peak serum levels are reached in 2 to 3 hours. It is not protein bound and is not metabolized; it is excreted unchanged in the urine. Elimination half-life averages 5 to 7 hours, which is not affected by repeated dosing. Gabapentin does not induce or inhibit hepatic enzymes, nor does it interact with other protein-bound drugs. Blood levels do not need to be monitored.

Dosing is recommended in a b.i.d. or t.i.d. schedule. Dosing usually starts at 300 mg/d, with titration occurring every 3 days in 300-mg increments to a usual dose of 900 mg/d, with a maximum dose of 3,600 mg/d. The dose must be adjusted for renally compromised patients.

Side effects include somnolence, dizziness, ataxia, fatigue, nystagmus, headache, tremor, and diplopia and mania in some cases. Most side effects tend to appear early and to be transient. A small percentage of patients do experience weight gain, which can be a compliance issue.

Lamotrigine

Lamotrigine is another newer anticonvulsant that has mood-stabilizing effects. It is available in 25-, 100-, 150-, and 200-mg tablets. It is well absorbed orally: peak serum levels are achieved in 1 to 5 hours. Food slightly delays the rate but not the extent of absorption. It is extensively metabolized to inactive metabolites in the liver. The mean half-life is approximately 24 hours, and 31 hours in the elderly. Levels have not been established for mood stabilization. Lamotrigine can be taken as a single daily dose or in a b.i.d. schedule. Dose should be initiated at 50 mg/d, and titrated by 50 mg/d every week or two to a dose range of 200 to 400 mg/d.

Adverse effects include nausea, headache, blurred vision, dizziness, ataxia, tremor, somnolence, and rash. Central nervous system (CNS) effects tend to occur early and to be transient, although they may be dose related, and occur more frequently when taken in combination with carbamazepine. Rash tends to be more common when lamotrigine is taken in combination with valproate. Rare cases of erythema multiforme, Stevens-Johnson syndrome, and toxic epidermal necrolysis have been described. Most rashes erupt within 6 weeks of therapy initiation, and resolve once the drug is discontinued.

Lamotrigine does not cause clinically significant induction or inhibition of the cytochrome P-450 system. Drugs that induce the P-450 system (eg, carbamazepine, phenytoin, and phenobarbital) decrease the half-life of lamotrigine by 50%. Valproate, however, lengthens the half-life of lamotrigine.

Selected Readings

Akiskal HS, Djenderedjian AM, Rosenthal RH, et al: Cyclothymic disorder: validating criteria for inclusion in the bipolar affective group. *Am J Psychiatry* 1977;134:1227-1233.

American Psychiatric Association: *Diagnostic and Statistical Manual of Mental Disorders*, 4th ed. Washington, DC, American Psychiatric Press, 1994.

Bowden CL, Janicak PG, Orsulak P, et al: Relation of serum valproate concentration to response in mania. *Am J Psychiatry* 1996;153:765-770.

Bowden CL, Brugger AM, Swann AC, et al: Efficacy of divalproex vs lithium and placebo in the treatment of mania. The Depakote Mania Study Group. *JAMA* 1994;271:918-924.

Burke KC, Burke JD, Regier DA, et al: Age at onset of selected mental disorders in five community populations. *Arch Gen Psychiatry* 1990;47:511-518.

Calabrese JR, Kimmel SE, Woyshville MJ, et al: Clozapine for treatment-refractory mania. *Am J Psychiatry* 1996;153:759-764.

Calabrese JR, Woyshville MJ, Kimmel SE, et al: Predictors of valproate response in bipolar rapid cycling. *J Clin Psychopharmacol* 1993;13:280-283.

Depakote and Depakene (valproate) product monograph. Abbott Laboratories.

Dubovsky SL, Buzan RD: Novel alternatives and supplements to lithium and anticonvulsants for bipolar affective disorder. *J Clin Psychiatry* 1997;58:224-242.

Dunner DL, Fieve RR: Clinical factors in lithium carbonate prophylaxis failure. *Arch Gen Psychiatry* 1974;30:229-233.

Eskalith (lithium carbonate) product monograph. SmithKline Beecham Pharmaceuticals.

Goodwin FK, Jamison KR: *Manic-Depressive Illness*. New York, Oxford University Press, 1990.

Janicak PG: The relevance of clinical pharmacokinetics and therapeutic drug monitoring: anticonvulsant mood stabilizers and antipsychotics. *J Clin Psychiatry* 1993;54:35-41.

Jefferson JW, Greist JH: Mood disorders. In: Hales RE, Yudofsky SC, Talbott JA, eds. *The American Psychiatric Press Textbook of Psychiatry*, 2nd ed. Washington DC, American Psychiatric Press, 1994.

Kukopulos A, Reginaldi D, Laddomada P, et al: Course of the manic-depressive cycle and changes caused by treatment. *Pharmakopsychiatr Neuropsychopharmakol* 1980;13:156-167.

Lamictal (lamotrigine) product monograph. Glaxo Wellcome.

Lithotabs (lithium carbonate) product monograph. Solvay Pharmaceuticals.

Medical Practice Information Demonstration Project: Bipolar disorder: A state-of-the-science report. Baltimore, MD, Policy Research Inc, 1979.

Neurontin (gabapentin) product monograph. Parke-Davis.

Physicians' Desk Reference, 51st ed. Montvale, NJ, Medical Economics Data Production Co, 1997.

Schaffer CB, Schaffer LC: Gabapentin in the treatment of bipolar disorder. *Am J Psychiatry* 1997;154:291-292.

Semenchuk MR, Labiner DM: Gabapentin and lamotrigine: prescribing guidelines for psychiatry. *J Pract Psychiatr Behav Health* 1997;3:334-342.

Small JG, Klapper MH, Milstein V, et al: Carbamazepine compared with lithium in the treatment of mania. *Arch Gen Psychiatry* 1991;48:915-921.

Sporn J, Sachs G: The anticonvulsant lamotrigine in treatment-resistant manic-depressive illness. *J Clin Psychopharmacol* 1997; 17:185-189.

Stewart DE, Klompenhouwer JL, Kendell RE, et al: Prophylactic lithium in puerperal psychosis. The experience of three centres. *Br J Psychiatry* 1991;158:393-397.

Suppes T, Baldessarini RJ, Faedda GL, et al: Risk of recurrence following discontinuation of lithium treatment in bipolar disorder. *Arch Gen Psychiatry* 1991;48:1082-1088.

Tegretol (carbamazepine) product monograph. Novartis.

Treatment of bipolar disorder. Steering Committee. The Expert Consensus Guideline Series. *J Clin Psychiatry* 1996;57:3-88.

Chapter 6

Chronic Depression, Bereavement, and Adjustment Disorder

C hronic depression can refer either to a major depressive episode that has not remitted (Chapter 4), or to dysthymia, which is a more chronic, less severe depressive disorder. Uncomplicated bereavement (as opposed to bereavement complicated by a major depression) is considered a normal reaction. As such, uncomplicated bereavement is not classified as a mental disorder. It refers to depressive symptoms that occur in response to the death of a loved one. An adjustment disorder with depressed mood refers to a maladaptive depressive reaction to an identifiable stressor or stressors occurring within 3 months after the onset of the stressor. This chapter addresses differential diagnosis as well as appropriate treatment approaches.

Dysthymia

Dysthymia is the presence of a chronically depressed mood occurring for most of the day for most days for at least 2 years (1 year for children and adolescents). In addition, at least two of the symptoms of major depressive disorder (change in appetite, change in sleep habits, low energy, low self-esteem, poor concentration, feelings of hopelessness) are present. Dysthymia has a lifetime prevalence rate of 6%, and affects females 1.5 to 3 times more than males. The onset of dysthymia usually is insidious and at an early age, and is chronic.

Dysthymia seldom exists alone; more than three quarters of patients have another condition, most commonly major depression (giving rise to a 'double depression'). Other comorbid disorders include anxiety disorders, substance abuse, personality disorders, conduct disorder, attention-deficit hyperactivity disorder, learning disorders, and mental retardation.

Case Report

RF was a 40-year-old, single, white, unemployed female, who was in the process of breaking up with her boyfriend when she sought treatment for depression that she said she had had 'all her life' but had become much worse. She described herself as never having been happy and had felt down and depressed for as long as she could remember. However, she also described 'dips' where she was more depressed than usual, unable to leave the house, feeling hopeless and helpless, with increased sleep and appetite. These 'dips' lasted for several weeks at a time and had occurred once or twice a year since her mid 20s. She had a history of getting into abusive relationships, changing jobs frequently, and feeling empty most of the time. She also had a history of cutting herself to feel better and of occasional binges on drugs and alcohol. Although she acknowledged they were bad for her, she claimed that these episodes did not coincide with her feeling depressed.

This patient had a double depression of both a major depressive disorder with atypical features and dysthymia. She also had comorbid borderline personality disorder and drug/alcohol abuse. She would probably benefit from a combination of antidepressant treatment (a selective serotonin reuptake inhibitor [SSRI] would be a good choice), rehabilitation for her substance abuse, and psychotherapy. Also, a mood stabilizer might be helpful if the impulsive/self-damaging behavior continued while on the SSRI.

Treatment of mild depressive disorders, including dysthymia, is mostly nonpharmacologic, and considered amenable to psychotherapy. However, antidepressant treatment, especially with the newer antidepressants such as SSRIs like fluoxetine (Prozac®), sertraline (Zoloft®), and the atypical antidepressant bupropion (Wellbutrin®), has been effective in a subgroup of patients. Because dysthymic symptoms can also cause considerable subjective distress, treatment with medications may be appropriate for these patients.

Uncomplicated Bereavement

Bereavement is a reaction to the loss of a loved one. Some grieving individuals can have symptoms characteristic of a major depressive episode, such as sadness, insomnia, poor appetite, and crying spells. The duration and expression of symptoms vary among cultures. However, episodes lasting longer than 2 months after the loss are classified as major depression. Symptoms that are not characteristic of uncomplicated bereavement include guilt other than survivor guilt, thoughts of death other than those connected to the survivor feeling that he or she should have died with the deceased, morbid preoccupation with worthlessness, significant psychomotor retardation, prolonged and significant functional impairment, hallucinations other than hearing the voice of the deceased or transiently seeing the image of the deceased, and serious suicidal thoughts or behavior.

In many cases, the preferred mode of treatment is psychotherapy aimed at helping the patient develop adequate coping skills for the loss. However, if the symptoms are severe and unremitting, antidepressant medications are a treatment option. Treatment with medication is similar to that used in the treatment of major depression, albeit for a much shorter duration. The length of treatment depends on rapidity of response and remission of symptoms. Indeed, patients can benefit much more from psychotherapy if their depressive symptoms are alleviated.

Adjustment Disorder

Adjustment disorder refers to the development of significant emotional or behavior symptoms in response to an identifiable stressor or stressors, developing within 3 months of the stress. Patients are unable to function, and suffer from distress in excess of that expected from the situation. An adjustment disorder that does not resolve within 6 months of the termination of the stressor is diagnosed as major depression. However, symptoms may persist for longer than 6 months in the case of a chronic stressor (eg, a chronic disabling medical condition) or an event that has long-lasting effects (eg, divorce). If the criteria for bereavement are met, the diagnosis of adjustment disorder cannot be made. The subtypes of adjustment disorder are: with depressed mood; with anxiety; with anxiety and depressed mood; with disturbance of conduct; and with mixed disturbance of emotions and conduct.

Adjustment disorders are associated with increased risk of suicide and suicide attempts. The presence of an adjustment disorder can often complicate the course of illness in individuals who have a general medical condition, such as by decreasing compliance or increasing length of stay. The prevalence of all adjustment disorders in an outpatient mental health setting ranges from 5% to 20%.

Treatment of adjustment disorders generally involves psychotherapy. However, in cases that are severe or cause significant complications, treatment with antidepressants is warranted. The doses used are similar to those used for major depression. Duration of treatment depends on response rate and symptom remission.

Selected Readings

American Psychiatric Association: *Diagnostic and Statistical Manual of Mental Disorders*, 4th ed. Washington, DC, American Psychiatric Press, 1994.

Grief and bereavement. *Psychiatr Clin North Am* 1987;10:329-515.

Hellerstein DJ, Yanowitch P, Rosenthal J, et al: A randomized double-blind study of fluoxetine versus placebo in the treatment of dysthymia. *Am J Psychiatry* 1993;150:1169-1175.

Howland RH, Thase ME: Biological studies of dysthymia. *Biol Psychiatry* 1991;30:283-304.

Jefferson JW, Greist JH: Mood disorders. In: Hales RE, Yudofsky SC, Talbott JA, eds. *The American Psychiatric Press Textbook of Psychiatry*, 2nd ed. Washington, DC, American Psychiatric Press, 1994.

Kocsis JH, Frances AJ: A critical discussion of DSM-III dysthymic disorder. *Am J Psychiatry* 1987;144:1534-1542.

Markowitz JC, Moran ME, Kocsis JH, et al: Prevalence and comorbidity of dysthymic disorder among psychiatric outpatients. *J Affect Disord* 1992;24:63-71.

Murphy DG: The classification and treatment of dysthymia. *Br J Psychiatry* 1991;158:106-109.

Rush AJ, Thase ME: Strategies and tactics in the treatment of chronic depression. *J Clin Psychiatry* 1997;58:14-22.

Sheldon F: ABC of palliative care. Bereavement. *BMJ* 1998; 316:456-458.

Thase ME, Fava M, Halbreich U, et al: A placebo-controlled, randomized clinical trial comparing sertraline and imipramine for the treatment of dysthymia. *Arch Gen Psychiatry* 1996;53:777-784.

Chapter **7**

Depression in Special Populations

S pecial populations of patients who suffer from depression may require treatment modifications because of differences in pharmacokinetics and pharmacodynamics, in comorbid medical conditions, and in how they respond to different treatments. This chapter addresses depression in three groups of patients: depression in the elderly, depression in pregnancy, and depression with a complicating comorbid medical condition such as myocardial infarction, stroke, or HIV infection.

Depression in the Elderly

Depression is one of the most frequent and disabling syndromes in geriatric psychiatry. Some researchers have suggested that the elderly are predisposed to depression by age-related structural and biochemical changes that may increase their vulnerability, by risk factors such as bereavement and other psychological losses, and by medical illness and institutionalization that become more common with age. The elderly also have a disproportionately high rate of suicide, about four times that of other major depression patients.

By conservative estimates, major depression occurs in 2% of the elderly, dysthymia in another 2%, and bipolar disorder in 0.2%. These numbers exclude patients suffering from adjustment disorder and bereavement.

Major depression is much more prevalent among older persons in hospitals and in long-term care facilities, ranging from 10% to 20%. Several studies have also found that depressive symptoms are much more prevalent in patients 80 years and older, and in older females compared with older males. Older people may have a different pattern of depressive symptoms from that found in earlier life, in particular, more somatic symptoms and fewer overt mood symptoms. As with other geriatric psychiatric syndromes, obtaining collaborative history from a family member is key to diagnosing depression in later life. Older persons are also more likely to exhibit psychotic symptoms during depressive episodes than are younger persons. Studies found that depressed men were significantly more pessimistic than depressed women. Depressed elderly patients also scored higher on scales for alexithymia (the inability to label one's own emotional state) and dysfunctional attitudes. In geriatric patients with major depression, recovery from a prior physical illness may increase the response rate to antidepressant therapy. However, in patients with severe baseline disability, response rate to antidepressant treatment may be decreased. In addition, depression was found to increase the likelihood of disability, predicting subsequent depression.

Comorbidity in the elderly with chronic major medical conditions (eg, cancer, myocardial infarction, Parkinson's disease, arthritis, hypertension, cerebrovascular accident, diabetes) is significant. In addition, many common medications, such as beta-blockers, can produce depressive symptoms. Therefore, a list of current medications should be reviewed.

In addition to thorough psychiatric and medical examinations, tests such as complete blood count (CBC), chemistry panel, Venereal Disease Research Laboratory (VDRL, a syphilis test), urinalysis, vitamin B_{12} and folate levels, thyroid panel, and an electrocardiogram are important screens for medical illness. Elective work-up includes brain imaging and polysomnography.

Treatment

Clinical management involves psychopharmacotherapy, electroconvulsive therapy (ECT), psychotherapy (especially cognitive and behavior therapies), and family education. We concentrate mostly on the biologic therapies (Table 1).

This population may have altered hepatic function, especially phase I reactions that include demethylation and hydroxylation, which are pathways that deactivate most antidepressants. In addition, renal function may be decreased, and end-organ sensitivity to medications may be increased. Elderly patients thus generally require much lower starting and endpoint therapeutic doses because of decreased clearance of these medications, and are more susceptible to side effects. Titration of medications should also be at a much slower rate than with younger patients.

Elderly patients generally tolerate the side effects of selective serotonin reuptake inhibitors (SSRIs), serotonin-norepinephrine reuptake inhibitors (SNRIs), and the other atypical antidepressants much better than tricyclic antidepressants (TCAs) and monoamine oxidase inhibitors (MAOIs). They tend to be especially sensitive to anticholinergic effects (which can cause constipation, urinary retention, and delirium), and adrenergic effects (which can cause orthostatic hypotension and, subsequently, falls). In addition, because TCAs are type 1A antiarrhythmics, TCAs are contraindicated in patients with known cardiac conditions because they would be at higher risk of developing conduction problems. In addition, elderly patients may generally be more sensitive to cardiac adverse events with TCA use. The most troublesome side effects of the serotonergic medications are agitation and weight loss. In addition, the more severe depressions with melancholic and psychotic features do not respond as well to the newer antidepressants as they do to TCAs or SNRIs. In these cases, ECT with proper medical support remains a safe and effective treatment for older adults, especially those with severe psychotic depressions.

The starting doses for geriatric patients are much lower than those used for healthy younger adults. In addition, the titration rate and therapeutic dosage range also are lower.

Depression During Pregnancy

Women experience depression at twice the rate of men. The child-bearing years are a time of increased risk for onset of depression in women. Up to 70% of pregnant women have had prior depressive symptoms, and 10% to 16% of women experience a major depression during pregnancy. Management of depression during pregnancy and the puerperium remains very challenging. The possibility of pregnancy and the effects of psychotropic medications must be considered at all times with female patients. Also, about half of all pregnancies are unplanned. Risk factors for depression during pregnancy include a patient or family history of depression, marital discord, recent adverse events, greater number of children, and unwanted pregnancy. The highest number of depressive symptoms occurred during weeks 34 through 38 of gestation. During pregnancy, volume expansion and increases in hepatic activity and renal clearance occur, and drug plasma levels may fall as the pregnancy progresses, resulting in increases in depressive symptoms.

Treatment

Treatment of depression during pregnancy includes psychotherapy, pharmacologic treatment, and ECT. ECT risk to the fetus is rare. The risks of untreated depression during pregnancy may include poor nutrition, difficulty following perinatal and medical recommendations, suicide, and increased use of tobacco, alcohol, or drugs.

Table 1: Pharmacologic Treatment of Geriatric Depression

Drug	Initial Dose (mg)	Usual Dosage Range (mg)	H_1-Histaminic Effects
imipramine	10	25-100	+++
nortriptyline	10	20-100	++
citalopram	10	20-40	0
fluoxetine	5	10-50	0
fluvoxamine	25	25-250	0
paroxetine	10	10-40	0
sertraline	25	25-150	0
bupropion	100	150-300	0
venlafaxine	50	50-225	0
mirtazapine	7.5-15	15-45	+++
nefazodone	100	100-400	0
trazodone	25	75-300	0

++++ = very strong effects;
+++ = strong effects;

Studies of teratogenicity of antidepressants during pregnancy are limited. Because we have more clinical experience with the TCAs, if a patient does need to be on a medication during pregnancy, this class may be preferred over the newer antidepressants. No increased risk of congenital malformations is associated with TCA use during pregnancy. Case reports about TCA withdrawal syndromes in neonates have been reported after TCA use during labor and delivery. These symptoms include jitteriness and irritability.

Alpha$_1$-Adrenergic Effects	Cardiac Conduction Delays	Overdose Lethality
+++	+++	++++
++	+++	++++
0	0	0
0	0	0
0	0	0
0	0	0
0	0	0
0	0	0
+	0	0
++	0	0
+++	0	0

++ = moderate effects;
+ = mild effects;
0 = minimal effects

Studies involving fluoxetine (Prozac®) showed no association with fetal malformations when used in the first trimester. The increased risk for perinatal complications was perhaps increased when taken in the third trimester, but this study is difficult to interpret because the study did not control for depression. A recent study with fluoxetine failed to find differences in IQ, language, and behavior after fetal exposure to the drug. Some of the newer SSRIs, fluvoxamine (Luvox®), paroxetine (Paxil®), and sertraline (Zoloft®), did not appear to increase the teratogenic risk at recommended doses. No studies have involved MAOIs, SNRIs, or other atypical antidepressants.

Of the mood stabilizers, lithium has an increased risk for development of cardiovascular malformations, most notably Ebstein's anomaly, in neonates exposed to it in utero during the first trimester. The risk of Ebstein's anomaly is 0.05% to 0.1%. Lithium exposure also is associated with the 'floppy baby' syndrome, characterized by cyanosis and hypotonicity. Other effects include neonatal hypothyroidism and nephrogenic diabetes insipidus. A study of children who had been exposed to lithium and who did not develop any malformations after a 5-year follow-up did not reveal any significant behavior problems. The risk of developing congenital malformations is increased after perinatal anticonvulsant exposure. Carbamazepine (Tegretol®) exposure during the first trimester is associated with spina bifida (1%). Valproic acid (Depakene®) has been associated with neural tube defects (3% to 5%). In addition, a syndrome of minor malformations characterized by rotated ears, flat nasal bridge, and fingernail hypoplasia has been described in infants exposed to anticonvulsants.

ECT has been found to be relatively safe and effective in the treatment of depression during pregnancy, with proper preparation. Limited data also show that antidepressants are excreted in breast milk, and information is inadequate on the effects of antidepressant medications in nursing infants. Therefore, nursing should be avoided if possible.

Postpartum Depression

The postpartum period has typically been considered a time of increased risk for mood disorders in women. At greatest risk are those women with histories of mood disorder and those who experience depression during pregnancy. Postpartum depressive disorders are often divided into three categories: (1) postpartum blues, (2) nonpsychotic postpartum depression, and (3) puerperal psychosis.

Postpartum blues is the most common of the three, with prevalence rates ranging from 30% to 75%. Characteristic symptoms include mood lability, irritability, tearfulness, anxiety, and sleep and appetite disturbance. Postpartum blues are time-limited and relatively benign. Symptoms usually peak at postpartum days 4 to 5, and remit by postpartum day 10.

Postpartum depression is also relatively common, with rates between 10% and 15%, similar to rates of depression in nonpuerperal cohorts. Although most women with postpartum depression have depressive symptoms within the first month after delivery, symptoms sometimes develop at the end of the pregnancy. The signs and symptoms are indistinguishable from those of major depression.

Postpartum psychosis is rare, occurring at rates between 0.1% to 0.2% after birth. The presentation is dramatic with onset as early as 2 to 3 days after delivery, with most developing within the first 2 weeks. Early symptoms include restlessness, irritability, and sleep disturbance. It then evolves to include either depressed or elated mood, mood lability, hallucinations, and delusions.

Treatment

Postpartum blues are time-limited and typically mild in severity. No specific treatment is indicated other than support and reassurance. Antidepressant medications, including sertraline, venlafaxine (Effexor®), and fluoxetine, have been used with some success to treat postpartum depression. Other treatments include estrogen, progesterone, cognitive-behavior therapy, and interpersonal psychotherapy. No current data suggest that postpartum depression should be managed any differently from nonpuerperal major depression. Postpartum psychosis is a psychiatric emergency and typically requires inpatient treatment. Acute treatment with mood stabilizers and antipsychotics is appropriate, as is ECT.

Depression in Medically Ill Patients

Depression often affects medically ill individuals, who can experience a major depressive disorder, an adjustment disorder with depression, or a depression attributable to their medical condition (eg, HIV disease, traumatic brain injury, cancer, stroke, lupus erythematosus). Medically ill populations tend to have special treatment concerns and issues. This section addresses depression in post-myocardial infarction patients, stroke patients, and HIV-infected patients.

Depression in Post-Myocardial Infarction Patients

Depression generally adversely affects the prognosis of patients with coronary artery disease (CAD). A history of depression has been found to increase the risk of myocardial infarction (MI). The prevalence in and prognostic impact on patients with MI showed that about 31% of patients experienced depression in the hospital or during the year postdischarge. A history of depression increased the risk of post-MI depression. Depression in the hospital was associated with increased risk of mortality over 18 months. Patients who experienced a recurrent depression in the hospital were at particular risk. The risk associated with depression has been found to be greatest in patients with more than or equal to 10 premature ventricular contractions (PVCs) an hour. The impact of post-MI depression on risk of mortality 6 months post-MI is thought to be at least equal to that of left ventricular dysfunction and previous MI.

Treatment

Treatment with psychotherapy, group therapy, and antidepressants has been shown to be helpful in MI patients. If a patient requires psychopharmacotherapy, the choice of antidepressant is very important. Studies in cardiology have demonstrated that the type 1A antiarrhythmics increased mortality rate when used in the post-MI population. Because tricyclics are classified as type 1A antiarrhythmics, the newer antidepressants, such as the SSRIs, SNRIs, and the atypical antidepressants, should be preferentially considered for the treatment of depression in MI patients because they lack arrhythmogenic effects.

Preliminary studies found that although nortriptyline (Pamelor®) and paroxetine were equally effective in treating depression in patients with CAD, nortriptyline was associated with a higher incidence of adverse cardiovascular events. The choice of antidepressant then depends on other factors (Chapter 4). Because many MI patients also have comorbid anxiety, the SSRIs are a good choice because they also have anxiolytic properties. Patients with significant cardiac problems (eg, recent MI, severe cardiac ischemia, significant hypertension) are more prone to the transient fluctuations in the cardiovascular system that occur during and shortly following ECT. Such patients must be thoroughly evaluated by a cardiologist familiar with the potential side effects of ECT if this treatment modality is to be considered.

Depression in Stroke Patients

Poststroke depression occurs in 22% to 60% of all Americans affected each year by strokes. Without intervention, the prevalence and severity of depression for these patients is highest between 6 months and 2 years poststroke. Poststroke depression is highly correlated with failure to resume premorbid social and physical activities. The severity of depression seems to correlate with proximity of the lesion to the left anterior frontal pole, and to subcortical lesions. Patients with marked poststroke depression tend to have more neurologic impairment, to have a history of depression, and to be female.

Treatment

Treatment comprises family support, education, and antidepressant medication. Patients who participate actively in programs designed for stroke victims tend to do better with regard to function and mental health. Antidepressant treatment has been shown to be effective for poststroke depression. Younger patients and those who have better social supports tend to do better with treatment. In addition, females tended to be less responsive than males in small studies. Choice of antidepressant is very important because stroke victims are very susceptible to side effects of psychotropic medications. TCAs are not recommended because of their many contraindications and adverse effects. Studies of SSRIs show good tolerability and effectiveness in the treatment of poststroke depression. Preliminary studies indicate that drugs with both noradrenergic and serotonergic effects (ie, the SNRIs) may be more effective. Stimulants such as dextroamphetamine (Dexedrine®) or methylphenidate (Ritalin®) are sometimes safe and effective in the treatment of poststroke depression. Case studies involving ECT show that it may be well tolerated in this group of patients. However, further studies are needed involving long-term effects and efficacy of treatment.

Depression in HIV Disease

Disturbances in mood, primarily depressive, but also manic and hypomanic episodes, occur in HIV disease. The depression in HIV patients has heterogeneous etiologies, but should never be considered normal in this population. The lifetime prevalence of depression in HIV-infected homosexual men is 30% to 45%. The rate was not found to be related to stage of illness. However, depression has been associated with an increased rate of decline of CD4 cell counts in HIV-infected persons. The relative risk of suicide in HIV-infected individuals is very high, up to 66 times that of the general population.

Treatment

Treatment of HIV patients with depression often involves a combination of psychotherapy and psychopharmacology. The HIV-infected brain is much more sensitive to medication response intensity and side effect development. Therefore, TCAs with fewer anticholinergic effects, and the newer antidepressants such as the SSRIs, including paroxetine and fluoxetine, SNRIs, and other atypical agents, have the least risk of producing side effects, affecting cognitive status, or causing delirium. The therapeutic dose of an antidepressant may be much lower in an HIV-infected person than for an uninfected person. Stimulants also have been helpful in the treatment of HIV-infected individuals, especially in those patients without any cognitive impairment. The usual dose of methylphenidate is 5 to 20 mg t.i.d. Depressed HIV-infected patients with psychotic symptoms or catatonia, or who have failed pharmacotherapy, may benefit from ECT. However, ECT can increase confusion in some patients with greater CNS involvement of the disease.

Selected Readings

Alexopoulos GS, Vrontou C, Kakuma T, et al: Disability in geriatric depression. *Am J Psychiatry* 1996;153:877-885.

Altshuler LL, Hendrick V, Cohen LS: Course of mood and anxiety disorders during pregnancy and the postpartum period. *J Clin Psychiatry* 1998;59:29-33.

Appleby L, Warner R, Whitton A, et al: A controlled study of fluoxetine and cognitive-behavioural counselling in the treatment of postnatal depression. *BMJ* 1997;314:932-936.

Atkinson JH Jr, Grant I, Kennedy CJ, et al: Prevalence of psychiatric disorders among men infected with human immunodeficiency virus. A controlled study. *Arch Gen Psychiatry* 1988;45:859-864.

Blazer D: Geriatric psychiatry. In: Hales RE, Yudofsky SC, Talbott JA, eds. *The American Psychiatric Press Textbook of Psychiatry*, 2nd ed. Washington, DC, American Psychiatric Press, 1994.

Blazer D: Depression in the elderly. *N Engl J Med* 1989;320:164-166.

Blazer DG, Hughes DC, George LJ: The epidemiology of anxiety depression in the elderly community population. *Gerontologist* 1987;27:281-287.

Bruce ML, Hoff RA: Social and physical health risk factors for first-onset major depressive disorder in a community sample. *Soc Psychiatry Psychiatr Epidemiol* 1994;29:165-171.

Burack JH, Barrett DC, Stall RD, et al: Depressive symptoms and CD4 lymphocyte decline among HIV-infected men. *JAMA* 1993; 270:2568-2573.

Chambers CD, Johnson KA, Dick LM, et al: Birth outcomes in pregnant women taking fluoxetine. *N Engl J Med* 1996;335: 1010-1015.

Chiou A, Potempa K, Buschmann MB: Anxiety, depression and coping methods of hospitalized patients with myocardial infarction in Taiwan. *Int J Nurs Stud* 1997;34:305-311.

Cleophas TJ: Depression and myocardial infarction. Implications for medical prognosis and options for treatment. *Drugs Aging* 1997;11:111-118.

Cohen LS: Treatment of psychiatric illness during pregnancy and the postpartum period. Presented at the annual meeting of the American Psychiatric Association, San Diego, 1997.

Cohen LS, Friedman JM, Jefferson JW, et al: A reevaluation of risk of in utero exposure to lithium. *JAMA* 1994;271:146-150.

Cohen LS, Rosenbaum JF: Psychotropic drug use during pregnancy: weighing the risks. *J Clin Psychiatry* 1998;59:18-28.

Dalton K: Progesterone prophylaxis used successfully in postnatal depression. *Practitioner* 1985;229:507-508.

Elliott AJ, Uldall KK, Bergam K, et al: Randomized, placebo-controlled trial of paroxetine versus imipramine in depressed HIV-positive outpatients. *Am J Psychiatry* 1998;155:367-372.

Fernandez F, Levy JK: Psychopharmacotherapy of psychiatric syndromes in asymptomatic and symptomatic HIV infection. *Psychiatr Med* 1991;9:377-394.

Fernandez F: Psychiatric complications in HIV-related illnesses. In: *American Psychiatric Association AIDS Primer*. Washington, DC, American Psychiatric Press, 1988.

Francisco GS: An overview of post-stroke depression. *N J Med* 1993;90:686-689.

Frasure-Smith N, Lesperance F, Talajic M: Depression and 18-month prognosis after myocardial infarction. *Circulation* 1995; 91:999-1005.

Frasure-Smith N, Lesperance F, Talajic M: Depression following myocardial infarction. Impact on 6-month survival. *JAMA* 1993; 270:1819-1825.

Glassman AH, Roose SP: Risks of antidepressants in the elderly: tricyclic antidepressants and arrhythmia-revising risks. *Gerontology* 1994;40:15-20.

Gregoire AJ, Kumar R, Everitt B, et al: Transdermal oestrogen for treatment of severe postnatal depression. *Lancet* 1996;347: 930-933.

Gustafson Y, Nilsson I, Mattsson M, et al: Epidemiology and treatment of post-stroke depression. *Drugs Aging* 1995;7:298-309.

Harrington C, Salloway S: The diagnosis and treatment of post-stroke depression. *Med Health R I* 1997;80:181-187.

Herrmann N, Black SE, Lawrence J, et al: The Sunnybrook Stroke Study: a prospective study of depressive symptoms and functional outcome. *Stroke* 1998;29:618-624.

Judd FK, Mijch AM, Cockram A: Fluoxetine treatment of depressed patients with HIV infection. *Aust N Z J Psychiatry* 1995;29: 433-436.

Katona C, Livingston G, Manela M, et al: The symptomatology of depression in the elderly. *Int Clin Psychopharmacol* 1997;12: S19-S23.

Katz IR, Simpson GM, Curlik SM, et al: Pharmacologic treatment of major depression for elderly patients in residential care settings. *J Clin Psychiatry* 1990;51:41-47.

Kendell RE, Chalmers JC, Platz C: Epidemiology of puerperal psychoses. *Br J Psychiatry* 1987;150:662-673.

Koenig HG, Meador KG, Cohen HJ, et al: Self-rated depression scales and screening for major depression in the older hospitalized patient with medical illness. *J Am Geriatr Soc* 1988;36: 699-706.

Kulin NA, Pastuszak A, Sage SR, et al: Pregnancy outcome following maternal use of the new selective serotonin reuptake inhibitors: a prospective controlled multicenter study. *JAMA* 1998; 279:609-610.

Lesperance F, Frasure-Smith N, Talajic M: Major depression before and after myocardial infarction: its nature and consequences. *Psychosom Med* 1996;58:99-110.

Lhagrissi-Thode F, Nelson CJ, Finkel MS, et al: Double-blind study of paroxetine versus nortriptyline in depressed patients with ischemic heart disease (abstract). *Psychopharmacol Bull* 1996;32:397.

Llewellyn A, Stowe ZN: Psychotropic medications in lactation. *J Clin Psychiatry* 1998;59:41-52.

Llewellyn AM, Stowe ZN, Nemeroff CB: Depression during pregnancy and the puerperium. *J Clin Psychiatry* 1997;58:26-32.

Marzuk PM, Tierney H, Tardiff K, et al: Increased risk of suicide in persons with AIDS. *JAMA* 1988;259:1333-1337.

Meyers BS, Bruce ML: Outcomes for antidepressant trials in late-life depression. *Psychopharmacol Bull* 1997;33:701-705.

Miller LJ: Use of electroconvulsive therapy during pregnancy. *Hosp Community Psychiatry* 1994;45:444-450.

Nonacs R, Cohen LS: Postpartum mood disorders: diagnosis and treatment guidelines. *J Clin Psychiatry* 1998;59:34-40.

Nulman I, Rovet J, Stewart DE, et al: Neurodevelopment of children exposed in utero to antidepressant drugs. *N Engl J Med* 1997; 336:258-262.

O'Hara MW, Zekoski EM, Phillipps LH, et al: Controlled prospective study of postpartum mood disorders: comparison of childbearing and nonchildbearing women. *J Abnorm Psychol* 1990;99: 3-15.

Omtzigt JG, Los FJ, Grobbee DE, et al: The risk of spina bifida aperta after first-trimester exposure to valproate in a prenatal cohort. *Neurology* 1992;42:119-125.

Palsson S, Skoog I: The epidemiology of affective disorders in the elderly: a review. *Int Clin Psychopharmacol* 1997;12:S3-S13.

Pastuszak A, Schick-Boschetto B, Zuber C, et al: Pregnancy outcome following first-trimester exposure to fluoxetine. *JAMA* 1993; 269:2246-2248.

Pitt B: 'Maternity blues'. *Br J Psychiatry* 1973;122:431-433.

Pratt LA, Ford DE, Crum RM, et al: Depression, psychotropic medication, and risk of myocardial infarction. Prospective data from the Baltimore ECA follow-up. *Circulation* 1996;94:3123-3129.

Roose SP, Glassman AH: Antidepressant choice in the patient with cardiac disease: lessons from the Cardiac Arrhythmia Suppression Trial (CAST) studies. *J Clin Psychiatry* 1994;55:83-87.

Rosa FW: Spina bifida in infants of women treated with carbamaze-pine during pregnancy. *N Engl J Med* 1991;324:674-677.

Schou M: Treating recurrent affective disorders during and after pregnancy. What can be taken safely? *Drug Saf* 1998;18:143-152.

Schou M: What happened later to the lithium babies? A follow-up study of children born without malformations. *Acta Psychiatr Scand* 1976;54:193-197.

Shima S: The efficacy of antidepressants in post-stroke depression. *Keio J Med* 1997;46:25-26.

Small GW, Birkett M, Meyers BS, et al: Impact of physical illness on quality of life and antidepressant response in geriatric major depression. Fluoxetine Collaborative Study Group. *J Am Geriatr Soc* 1996;44:1220-1225.

Stowe ZN, Casarella J, Landrey J, et al: Sertraline in the treatment of women with postpartum major depression. *Depression* 1995; 3:49-55.

Stuart S, O'Hara MW: Interpersonal psychotherapy for postpar-tum depression: a treatment program. *J Psychother Pract Res* 1995;4:18-29.

Tiller JW: Post-stroke depression. *Psychopharmacology (Berl)* 1992;106:S130-S133.

Walker R, Swartz CM: Electroconvulsive therapy during high-risk pregnancy. *Gen Hosp Psychiatry* 1994;16:348-353.

Chapter 8

Refractory Depression

Treatment-refractory depression is depression that fails to respond to conventional antidepressant treatment. However, before a patient is labeled treatment resistant or treatment refractory, the clinician must evaluate whether the patient has received adequate treatment with an antidepressant with regard to dosage, duration, and compliance. An adequate trial requires that the patient be maintained on the maximum tolerated dose of the antidepressant for at least 6 weeks. In addition, reevaluation may reveal depressive subtypes that may be more responsive to certain classes of medications, or the presence of comorbid psychiatric illness, which could require a different choice of medication or augmentation with a second drug for maximum benefit. If the patient does not respond to the initial antidepressant, strategies can be implemented to maximize efficacy. This chapter addresses the definition of treatment nonresponse and augmentation strategies for treatment-refractory depression.

Defining Antidepressant Nonresponse

Patients may not respond to antidepressant treatment for several reasons. The most common reason is incorrect diagnosis. In patients with 'double depression' (eg, major depression and dysthymia), symptoms related to the major depression often improve with antidepressant treatment, but those related to dysthymia may not. In addition, patients with comorbid substance or alcohol abuse improve with regard to their major depression, but problems with their abuse persist, including mood symptoms.

Another prevalent reason for antidepressant nonresponse is noncompliance. Some patients fear the side effects, while others are afraid of developing a dependence on the medication. Still others take the medication on an as-needed basis (prn). Compliance can be checked by monitoring drug levels when the patient does not seem to respond to treatment. Medication counseling and the use of newer antidepressants with more favorable side effect profiles should improve patient compliance and decrease treatment failures.

Subtherapeutic dosage is another common reason for treatment nonresponse. Studies have shown that patients are prescribed insufficient doses of tricyclic antidepressants (TCAs) about half the time. Therefore, for patients who still respond suboptimally, the tolerated dose must be titrated up to the maximum recommended dose, if possible, before calling the trial a failure.

Duration of the antidepressant trial also is important. Traditionally, nonresponse is defined as no clinical response occurring after 6 weeks of an adequate dose of a medication. Although many patients begin to respond after 2 to 3 weeks, some may not show signs of improvement until weeks 5 or 6.

A rare reason for treatment nonresponse is malabsorption of the medication, such as that occurring in inflammatory bowel disease, or in those patients who have undergone partial surgical resection of the bowel. Also, patients who are rapid metabolizers of antidepressants can have low blood levels of the active metabolite.

Concurrent medical illness, especially mood disorder from medical illness, is a complicating factor that can result in treatment nonresponse. Therefore, the underlying medical problem should be addressed as well to optimize treatment response. This is especially true for patients with hypothyroidism, where thyroid function tests (TFTs) must be normalized before an adequate response to antidepressants occurs.

Mood symptoms related to medications such as antihypertensives (eg, reserpine, propranolol [Inderal®], calcium-channel blockers) also can lead to treatment nonresponse. In addition, a positive response can be lost in patients already on an antidepressant medication who are subsequently given an antihypertensive that negates the effects of the antidepressant drug.

Case Report

GR was a 25-year-old, married, unemployed investment banker living at home with her husband of 9 months. She was referred for a consultation. She had a history of depression since her late teens and had been treated with multiple medications, including sertraline (Zoloft®), paroxetine (Paxil®), desipramine (Norpramin®), venlafaxine (Effexor®), with augmentors such as clonazepam (Klonopin®), alprazolam (Xanax®), and lithium (Lithobid®). She discontinued the lithium because of weight gain. All of the different regimens had only minimal effect. After her marriage, she developed recurrent panic attacks without agoraphobia. Her depressive symptoms also increased in severity, with marked neurovegetative symptoms, and led to losing her job. She also had a history of anorexia nervosa that reemerged after her marriage. Her weight had decreased from a baseline of 118 lb to 95 lb (she was 5-ft-7-in tall). She was then placed on a regimen of fluoxetine (Prozac®), clonazepam up to 4 mg/d, alprazolam up to 6 mg/d, and trazodone (Desyrel®) for sleep. In addition, she was found to have abnormal TFTs and was placed on thyroid replacement therapy, which was discontinued because of her continued weight loss. Her oral contraceptive pills were also discontinued. The fluoxetine was tapered because of its anorexic effects, all resulting in a worsening of her depressive and anxiety symptoms. On evaluation, it was discovered that her eating disorder was severe and

> ## Table 1: Strategies for Refractory Depression
>
> - Change antidepressants, preferably to a different class of antidepressants, eg, from an SSRI to an SNRI such as venlafaxine (Effexor®)
>
> - Augmentation, eg, with thyroid hormone (T_3; Cytomel®), mood stabilizers (such as lithium [Eskalith®, Lithonate®, Lithobid®]), buspirone (BuSpar®), stimulants (such as dextroamphetamine [Dexedrine®]), benzodiazepines (such as clonazepam [Klonopin®]), antipsychotics (such as risperidone [Risperdal®]), or pindolol (Visken®)
>
> - Combination antidepressant therapy (eg, fluoxetine [Prozac®] + bupropion [Wellbutrin®])
>
> - Electroconvulsive therapy (ECT) (Chapter 2)
>
> - Neurosurgery (Chapter 2)

she was in denial about it, refusing to get any therapy. In addition, laboratory tests found that she had amphetamines, benzodiazepines, and cocaine metabolites in her urine.

This is a complicated case. The patient was probably initially refractory to depression treatment because of the undiagnosed active eating disorder and probable abuse of amphetamines, benzodiazepines, and cocaine. In addition, the abnormal thyroid function and hormonal factors in the latest depressive episode cannot be dismissed entirely as contributing factors as well, nor can the development of panic disorder. The recommendations for subsequent treatment included rehabilitation for substance abuse; specific therapies addressing her depressive, panic, and eating disorders; reevaluation of her thyroid function and treatment if abnormal; re-titration of the SSRI she was taking and consideration of augmenting it with a mood stabilizer such as valproate (Depakote®), or buspirone (BuSpar®), or a combination with a different class of antidepressant, such as bupropion (Wellbutrin®) or a tricyclic agent. However, the combination of an SSRI and bupropion should be used cautiously in a patient with an active eating disorder because of the risk of seizure.

Strategies to maximize treatment with refractory depression are listed in Table 1.

Augmentation With Thyroid Hormone

Among depressed patients, the rates of subtle thyroid dysfunction (eg, autoimmune thyroiditis, alterations in pituitary secretion of thyroid-stimulating hormone [TSH]) are much higher than in nondepressed patients. Augmentation with T_3 (liothyronine; Cytomel®) rather than T_4 (levothyroxine; Synthroid®) led to significantly greater response rates. Studies have shown good results when T_3 was used to augment TCA and selective serotonin reuptake inhibitor (SSRI) effects. About 30% of nonresponders became responders after addition of T_3. Doses of T_3 range from 25 to 50 mg/d. Some improvement usually is seen within 2 to 4 weeks of treatment. Female patients with prominent fatigue and psychomotor retardation tended to respond most optimally to T_3 augmentation to SSRIs. T_3 augmentation does not seem to increase plasma levels of the TCAs.

Augmentation With Lithium and Other Mood Stabilizers

The addition of lithium (Eskalith®, Lithobid®, Lithonate®) to antidepressant regimens has been successful in converting nonresponders to responders in about 60% of cases. Augmentation with lithium to TCAs, monoamine oxidase inhibitors (MAOIs), and SSRIs has been shown to improve depressive symptoms. Augmentation doses of lithium range from 300 to 900 mg/d. Patients who respond do so over a range of drug levels, usually after several days to weeks of treatment. The plasma range of lithium most associated with treatment response has not been determined, if any exists.

Few controlled studies have examined augmentation with mood stabilizers other than lithium. Clinical reports have shown improvement in some patients when mood stabilizers such as carbamazepine (Tegretol®) and valproate (valproic acid; Depakene®) were added to antidepressant monotherapy. Dosage range depends on clinical response and side effect tolerability.

Patients with comorbid impulsive disorders or impulsive personalities also may benefit from augmentation with mood stabilizers.

Augmentation With Buspirone

Trials of augmentation of SSRIs with buspirone have shown improvement in depressive symptoms during 4 weeks of treatment in doses of up to 45 mg/d. In addition, in patients with significant comorbid anxiety, this regimen may be helpful in treating the anxiety symptoms as well.

Augmentation With Stimulants

Trials of stimulant augmentation to antidepressants have shown to be helpful in a subset of treatment-refractory patients. Although stimulants may raise levels of the antidepressant, the effects tend to be more related to their dopaminergic properties. Subgroups of patients who tend to respond better to stimulant augmentation include medically ill patients with psychomotor retardation (eg, after cerebrovascular accident, HIV infection). Stimulant use has not shown to cause dependence when used as an augmentation strategy; however, stimulants should not be used in patients with a history of substance or alcohol abuse or dependence. Other subgroups of patients who should not receive stimulants include those with agitation and insomnia, especially those taking SSRIs, and those prone to psychosis. Effective stimulant doses are usually determined empirically, but typically range from 2.5 to 10 mg/d of dextroamphetamine (Dexedrine®) or 20 to 60 mg/d of methylphenidate (Ritalin®).

Augmentation With Benzodiazepines

Treatment-refractory patients with significant anxiety symptoms may respond to benzodiazepine augmentation. Benzodiazepines with longer half-lives, such as clonazepam, are preferable to decrease peak and trough effects, and reduce feelings of immediate 'highs' that may encourage abuse. These are generally easier to taper and discontinue in the future, if necessary.

Augmentation With Antipsychotics

Treatment-refractory patients with psychotic symptoms respond well to the addition of an antipsychotic medication. Patients with comorbid cluster A personality disorders (eg, schizotypal, schizoid, paranoid) or borderline personality disorder may benefit from antipsychotic augmentation.

Augmentation With Pindolol

Augmentation strategies using pindolol, a beta-blocker with 5-HT_{1A} antagonist effects, with SSRIs such as fluoxetine and paroxetine, MAOIs such as tranylcypromine (Parnate®), and nefazodone (Serzone®) have been reported with some success and with a faster onset of antidepressant effects. The dose of pindolol used for augmentation is 7.5 mg/d in divided doses (2.5 mg t.i.d.). However, more studies are needed.

Antidepressant Combination Therapy

Combinations of antidepressants may be used to treat refractory depression. Antidepressants from two different classes usually are combined to maximize effectiveness by targeting different neurotransmitter systems. Combining two antidepressants usually increases the blood levels of one or both and, therefore, careful monitoring of drug levels, especially of the TCAs, is needed to prevent adverse and toxic effects, such as seizures.

Case reports and open trials show that combinations of a TCA such as desipramine (Norpramin®) or nortriptyline (Pamelor®) with an SSRI, or bupropion, have been helpful in treatment-refractory depression. Further studies are needed to test the efficacy of combinations, and to study long-term effects. Combinations of an SSRI with either bupropion or mirtazapine (Remeron®) also have been reported to be helpful. Other combinations with the newer antidepressants have not yet been studied.

Selected Readings

Apter JT, Kushner SF, Woolfolk RL: Bupropion/nortriptyline combination for refractory depression. *Ann Clin Psychiatry* 1994;6: 255-258.

Bakish D, Hooper CL, Thornton MD, et al: Fast onset: an open study of the treatment of major depressive disorder with nefazodone and pindolol combination therapy. *Int Clin Psychopharmacol* 1997;12:91-97.

Birkenhager TK, Vegt M, Nolen WA: An open study of triiodothyronine augmentation of tricyclic antidepressants in inpatients with refractory depression. *Pharmacopsychiatry* 1997;30:23-26.

Bouwer C, Stein DJ: Buspirone is an effective augmenting agent of serotonin selective re-uptake inhibitors in severe treatment-refractory depression. *S Afr Med J* 1997;87:534-537.

de Montigny C: Lithium addition in treatment-resistant depression. *Int Clin Psychopharmacol* 1994;9:31-35.

Feiner NF: Antiepileptic drug augmentation for treatment-resistant depression. *J Clin Psychiatry* 1997;58:361-363.

Henry JA, Hale AS: Selective serotonin reuptake inhibitors. Unsuccessful treatment may be related to non-response or non-compliance. *BMJ* 1994;309:1083.

Hullett FJ, Potkin SG, Levy AB, et al: Depression associated with nifedipine-induced calcium channel blockade. *Am J Psychiatry* 1988;145:1277-1279.

Joffe RT, Levitt AJ, Sokolov ST: Augmentation strategies: focus on anxiolytics. *J Clin Psychiatry* 1996;57:25-31.

Kraus RP: Pindolol augmentation of tranylcypromine in psychotic depression. *J Clin Psychopharmacol* 1997;17:225-226.

Lin EH, Von Korff M, Katon W, et al: The role of the primary care physician in patients' adherence to antidepressant therapy. *Med Care* 1995;33:67-74.

Nemeroff CB: Augmentation regimens for depression. *J Clin Psychiatry* 1991;52:21-27.

Nemeroff CB: Augmentation strategies in patients with refractory depression. *Depress Anxiety* 1996;4:169-181.

O'Connor M, Silver H: Adding risperidone to selective serotonin reuptake inhibitor improves chronic depression. *J Clin Psychopharmacol* 1998;18:89-91.

Perez V, Gilaberte I, Faries D, et al: Randomised, double-blind, placebo-controlled trial of pindolol in combination with fluoxetine antidepressant treatment. *Lancet* 1997;349:1594-1597.

Preskorn SH: Tricyclic antidepressants: the whys and hows of therapeutic drug monitoring. *J Clin Psychiatry* 1989;50:34-42.

Roose ST, Glassman AH, Walsh BT, et al: Tricyclic nonresponders: phenomenology and treatment. *Am J Psychiatry* 1986;143:345-348.

Schweitzer I, Tuckwell V, Johnson G: A review of the use of augmentation therapy for the treatment of resistant depression: implications for the clinician. *Aust N Z J Psychiatry* 1997;31:340-352.

Stoll AL, Pillay SS, Diamond L, et al: Methylphenidate augmentation of serotonin selective reuptake inhibitors: a case series. *J Clin Psychiatry* 1996;57:72-76.

Tome MB, Isaac MT, Harte R, et al: Paroxetine and pindolol: a randomized trial of serotonergic autoreceptor blockade in the reduction of antidepressant latency. *Int Clin Psychopharmacol* 1997;12:81-89.

Section III: Anxiety: Diagnosis and Management

Chapter **9**

Anxiety: Overview and Diagnosis

A nxiety disorders are the most common psychiatric illnesses, affecting some 26.9 million Americans at some point during their lives. Anxiety disorders result in significant functional impairment and distress. In 1990, costs associated with anxiety disorders were estimated at $46.6 billion, accounting for 31.5% of the total expenditures for mental illness. More than 75% of costs were attributable to lost or reduced productivity.

Anxiety disorders include panic disorder, social and specific phobias, generalized anxiety disorder, obsessive-compulsive disorder, and posttraumatic stress disorder. Most patients respond to appropriate treatment, and are able to return to their previous level of functioning. Anxiety is a prominent component of other psychiatric diagnoses as well, including agitated depression, delirium, dementia, schizophrenia, and obsessive-compulsive related disorders (eg, pathologic gambling [an impulse control disorder], body dysmorphic disorder [a somatoform disorder], and autism [a pervasive developmental disorder with significant neurologic involvement]). Medical conditions such as thyroid abnormalities, mitral valve prolapse, cardiac arrhythmias, hypoglycemia, and vertigo, as well as drug and alcohol use or withdrawal, also often result in anxiety (Table 1), and should be included in the differential diagnoses. In addition, many common drugs

Table 1: Medical Conditions Associated With Anxiety

- Alzheimer's disease
- cardiac arrhythmias
- cerebrovascular accident
- CNS tumors near third ventricle
- hypoglycemia
- mitral valve prolapse
- Parkinson's disease
- pheochromocytoma
- seizure disorder: ictal and postictal periods
- subarachnoid hemorrhage
- thyroid dysfunction
- vertigo

can produce anxiety symptoms (Table 2). Therefore, the identification of anxiety symptoms should lead to the diagnosis of the particular anxiety syndrome and, subsequently, to appropriate and specific treatment.

Symptoms of extreme anxiety include subjective feelings of tension and jitteriness, excessive worrying, irritability, restlessness, difficulty concentrating, sleep disturbance, and somatic symptoms such as palpitations, choking, trembling, dizziness, fatigue, dyspnea, chest pain, and autonomic signs of sweating. Symptoms of increased arousal, such as an exaggerated startle response and hypervigilance, may be present. Symptoms may also include cognitive dysfunction, such as inattention and problems with concentration. Specific anxiety terms are defined in Table 3.

In addition, people who experience anxiety tend to avoid situations or stimuli associated with the anxiety. For example, people who suffer from posttraumatic stress disorder avoid situations that arouse recollections of the trauma, and those who suffer from panic attacks tend not to want to leave the house, or avoid situations where they might be trapped or where help might not be available if they experience a panic attack.

When diagnosing anxiety, after excluding medical conditions and the effects of a substance that may be causing the symptoms, the clinician should determine if the patient has:

- panic attacks with or without agoraphobia (panic disorder)
- fear of humiliation in social or performance situations (social phobia)
- fear cued by an object or situation (specific phobia)
- obsessions or compulsions (obsessive-compulsive disorder and related disorders)
- excessive worrying and anxiety about everyday life situations (generalized anxiety disorder)
- anxiety in response to a severe traumatic event (posttraumatic stress disorder).

Table 3: Definition of Anxiety Terms

Phobia: a persistent, irrational fear of an object, activity, or situation that results in avoidance behavior

Obsessions: recurrent and persistent thoughts, impulses, or images that are intrusive and inappropriate, and that cause marked anxiety and distress

Compulsions: repetitive behaviors that a person feels driven to perform to prevent or reduce anxiety and distress

Panic attacks: discrete periods of intense fear or discomfort that develop abruptly and reach a peak within 10 minutes. Symptoms include at least four of the following: palpitations, sweating, trembling, shortness of breath or choking, chest pain, nausea, dizziness, derealization (feelings of unreality) or depersonalization (being detached from oneself), fear of losing control, paresthesias (numbness or tingling sensations), and hot or cold flushes.

Treatment of the different disorders usually includes pharmacotherapy or psychotherapy, such as cognitive-behavior, insight-oriented, and supportive psychotherapies, if symptoms are severe and disabling enough. Medications include anxiolytics, such as benzodiazepines or buspirone (BuSpar®), and antidepressants, such as the selective serotonin reuptake inhibitors (SSRIs), tricyclic antidepressants (TCAs), monoamine oxidase inhibitors (MAOIs) (Chapter 2), and beta-blockers, such as propranolol (Inderal®). Several anxiety disorders are addressed in greater detail in the following chapters, including both diagnostic and treatment issues.

Selected Readings

American Psychiatric Association: *Diagnostic and Statistical Manual of Mental Disorders*, 4th ed. Washington, DC, American Psychiatric Association, 1994.

Beck AT, Emery G, Greenberg RL: *Anxiety Disorders and Phobias: A Cognitive Perspective*. New York, Basic Books, 1985.

DuPont RL, Rice DP, Miller LS, et al: Economic costs of anxiety disorders. *Anxiety* 1996;2:167-172.

Hollander E, Simeon D, Gorman JM: Anxiety disorders. In: Hales RE, Yudofsky SC, Talbott JA, eds. *The American Psychiatric Press Textbook of Psychiatry*, 2nd ed. Washington, DC, American Psychiatric Press, 1994.

Noyes R, Roth M, Burrows GD, eds. *Handbook of Anxiety, Vol. 4: The Treatment of Anxiety*. New York, Elsevier, 1990.

Strub RL, Wise MG: Differential diagnosis in neuropsychiatric disorders. In: Yudofsky SC, Hales RE, eds. *The American Psychiatric Press Textbook of Neuropsychiatry*, 3rd ed. Washington, DC, American Psychiatric Press, 1997.

Chapter 10

Generalized Anxiety Disorder

The essential features of generalized anxiety disorder (GAD) are excessive anxiety and worry occurring more days than not over at least 6 months. Patients with GAD often have significant impairment in quality of life. These patients also have been found to have increased economic dependence, multiple somatic complaints, maladaptive personality traits, and increased rate of mortality.

Patients experience great difficulty in controlling the worry, and the anxiety is accompanied by at least three of the following: feelings of restlessness, difficulty concentrating, irritability, disturbed sleep, and muscle tension. The anxiety focuses on a number of everyday events or activities. The intensity and duration of the worry is far out of proportion to the actual likelihood or impact of the feared event, resulting in significant functional impairment. Adults with GAD often worry about everyday, routine events such as job responsibilities, finances, health of family members, their children, household chores, being late for appointments, etc. Children with GAD tend to worry about their school performance and grades, competence, punctuality, and catastrophic events. During the course of the worry, the focus can shift from one subject to another.

GAD is twice as common in women than in men. The 1-year prevalence is approximately 3%, with a lifetime prevalence rate of 5%. Onset of the disorder often occurs in childhood, although symptoms emerging in the 20s are not uncommon. The course of illness is chronic and often exacerbated by stress. Patients with GAD often also have depressive symptoms, such as hopelessness, frustration, and demoralization. Abuse of alcohol, barbiturates, and antianxiety medications may also be common in these patients. The comorbidity of chronic depression with GAD is very high. In addition, some GAD patients have histories of occasional panic attacks. The differential diagnoses of GAD are outlined in Table 1.

Case Report

JB was a 32-year-old, married female with two small children. She sought psychiatric treatment after the school counselor of her older child suggested that she get professional counseling. Her older son had been having behavioral and attention problems and was directed to the school counselor, who elicited from the child that his mother was always upset with him and yelling at him, making him feel that he could not do anything right. JB reported that she was always anxious, especially about her children, always worrying that they were all right, that they did their homework and cleaned their rooms, and that they were able to keep to their schedules. These concerns were apart from other everyday worries she had about herself, her husband, her mother-in-law, and the maid. She directed the anxiety mostly at her husband and children, and she would get so anxious and frustrated that she would yell at them for no reason. She felt 'wound up,' was restless and tense, had difficulty concentrating, and slept poorly. Her marriage and family relationships had deteriorated as a result. After a clinician spoke with JB and her husband, she entered treatment. Her symptoms were successfully controlled with a 20-mg/d dose of fluoxetine (Prozac®). She is undergoing psychotherapy to deal with other issues and her coping mechanisms. Her children are doing

Table 1: Differential Diagnoses of Generalized Anxiety Disorder

- Anxiety from a general medical condition

- Substance-induced anxiety disorder

- Panic disorder (worrying restricted to or following panic attacks)

- Social phobia (anxiety restricted to being embarrassed or humiliated in public)

- Obsessive-compulsive disorder (obsessions are intrusive and often ego-dystonic, restricted to certain areas such as contamination or symmetry, and concerns are less realistic than in GAD)

- Anorexia nervosa (anxiety restricted to gaining weight)

- Hypochondriasis (anxiety restricted to having a serious illness)

- Somatization disorder (anxiety restricted to multiple physical complaints)

- Posttraumatic stress disorder (anxiety related to a certain stressful event)

- Adjustment disorder (anxiety related to a stressor that does not persist for more than 6 months after the termination of the stressor)

- Mood disorders (anxiety is a common associated feature, such as anxious depression)

- Psychotic disorders (anxiety is also a very common feature of the illness)

- Nonpathologic anxiety (no distress or interference with functioning) better in school, and her husband has agreed to couples therapy.

Treatment

Treatment options include pharmacotherapy and psychotherapy, such as insight-oriented and cognitive-behavior approaches. No study has found that any one modality of treatment is significantly more effective than any other. Pharmacologic treatment centers on benzodiazepines, buspirone (BuSpar®), tricyclic antidepressants (TCAs) such as amitriptyline (Elavil®), selective serotonin reuptake inhibitors (SSRIs) such as paroxetine (Paxil®) and fluoxetine, atypical antidepressants (eg, nefazodone [Serzone®]), and serotonin-norepinephrine reuptake inhibitors (SNRIs) (eg, venlafaxine [Effexor® XR]), which recently received an FDA indication for GAD. Some studies have found similar efficacy for alprazolam (Xanax®) and imipramine (Tofranil®), with alprazolam being more effective in treating somatic symptoms, and imipramine being more effective in targeting psychic symptoms. Researchers also have suggested that benzodiazepines peak in effectiveness after 4 weeks of treatment, whereas TCAs may be more effective over the long term. SSRIs and SNRIs have a more favorable side effect profile compared with the tricyclics, and our experience has also shown that patients tolerate the SSRIs and SNRIs better, and thus are more compliant with treatment.

Buspirone has a better side effect profile than benzodiazepines and tricyclic antidepressants, because it has no withdrawal or rebound effects. The disadvantage, however, is a slower onset of action, which can often lead to early noncompliance. Buspirone has been found to have a similar efficacy to clorazepate (Tranxene®), a benzodiazepine. Researchers also have suggested that patients treated previously with benzodiazepines may not respond as well to buspirone.

Other medications being studied for use in GAD include abecarnil, a partial benzodiazepine-receptor agonist; ondansetron (Zofran®), a 5-HT$_3$ agent; and 5-HT$_1$ agonists such as ipsapirone, gepirone, and flesinoxan. These drugs have not yet been approved for use in anxiety disorders.

Selected Readings

American Psychiatric Association: *Diagnostic and Statistical Manual of Mental Disorders*, 4th ed. Washington, DC, American Psychiatric Association, 1994.

Blazer DG, Hughes D, George LK: Generalized anxiety disorder. In: Robins LN, Regier DA, eds. *Psychiatric Disorders in America.* New York, Free Press, 1991.

Breslau N, Davis GC: DSM-III generalized anxiety disorder: an empirical investigation of more stringent criteria. *Psychiatry Res* 1985;15:231-238.

Fairbanks JM, Pine DS, Tancer NK, et al: Open fluoxetine treatment of mixed anxiety disorders in children and adolescents. *J Child Adolesc Psychopharmacol* 1997;7:17-29.

Freeman AM 3rd, Westphal JR, Norris GT, et al: Efficacy of ondansetron in the treatment of generalized anxiety disorder. *Depress Anxiety* 1997;5:140-141.

Hoehn-Saric R, McLeod DR, Zimmerli WD: Differential effects of alprazolam and imipramine in generalized anxiety disorder: somatic versus psychic symptoms. *J Clin Psychiatry* 1988;49:293-301.

Hollander E, Simeon D, Gorman JM: Anxiety disorders. In: Hales RE, Yudofsky SC, Talbott JA, eds. *American Psychiatric Textbook of Psychiatry*, 2nd ed. Washington, DC, American Psychiatric Press, 1994.

Kahn RJ, McNair DM, Lipman RS, et al: Imipramine and chlordiazepoxide in depressive and anxiety disorders. II. Efficacy in anxious outpatients. *Arch Gen Psychiatry* 1986;43:79-85.

Lydiard RB, Ballenger JC, Rickels K: A double-blind evaluation of the safety and efficacy of abecarnil, alprazolam, and placebo in outpatients with generalized anxiety disorder. Abecarnil Work Group. *J Clin Psychiatry* 1997;58:11-18.

Mandos LA, Rickels K, Cutler N, et al: Placebo-controlled comparison of the clinical effects of rapid discontinuation of ipsapirone and lorazepam after 8 weeks of treatment for generalized anxiety disorder. *Int Clin Psychopharmacol* 1995;10:251-256.

Massion AO, Warshaw MG, Keller MB: Quality of life and psychiatric morbidity in panic disorder and generalized anxiety disorder. *Am J Psychiatry* 1993;150:600-607.

Pollack MH, Worthington JJ, Manfro GG, et al: Abecarnil for the treatment of generalized anxiety disorder: a placebo-controlled comparison of two dosage ranges of abecarnil and buspirone. *J Clin Psychiatry* 1997;58:19-23.

Pounds R: A review of the medical and social consequences of generalized anxiety disorder and panic disorder. *J La State Med Soc* 1992;144:479-483.

Rickels K, Csanalosi I, Chung HR, et al: Amitriptyline in anxious-depressed outpatients: a controlled study. *Am J Psychiatry* 1974; 131:25-30.

Rickels K, Schweizer E, Csanalosi I, et al: Long-term treatment of anxiety and risk of withdrawal. Prospective comparison of clorazepate and buspirone. *Arch Gen Psychiatry* 1988;45:444-450.

Rickels K, Schweitzer E, DeMartinis N, et al: Gepirone and diazepam in generalized anxiety disorder: a placebo-controlled trial. *J Clin Psychopharmacol* 1997;17:272-277.

Rocca P, Fonzo V, Scotta M, et al: Paroxetine efficacy in the treatment of generalized anxiety disorder. *Acta Psychiatr Scand* 1997;95:444-450.

Rodgers RJ, Cole JC, Davies A: Antianxiety and behavioral suppressant actions of the novel $5-HT_{1A}$ receptor agonist, flesinoxan. *Pharmacol Biochem Behav* 1994;48:959-963.

Schweizer E, Rickels K, Lucki I: Resistance to the anti-anxiety effect of buspirone in patients with a history of benzodiazepine use. *N Engl J Med* 1986;314:719-720.

Shammas E: Controlled comparison of bromazepam, amitriptyline, and placebo in anxiety-depressive neurosis. *Dis Nerv Syst* 1977;38: 201-207.

Chapter **11**

Panic Disorder

P anic disorder is characterized by the presence of recurrent, unexpected panic attacks, or a single panic attack followed by at least 1 month of persistent concern about having another panic attack, worry about the possible implications or consequences of the panic attacks, or a significant change in behavior related to the attacks. At least two unexpected, spontaneous attacks that are not associated with any trigger are required to diagnose panic disorder, although situationally bound panic attacks are also very common. Panic attacks are defined in Chapter 9.

Significant quality-of-life issues affect patients with panic disorder. The unemployment rate among these patients was 25% in one study, and only 57% of panic patients were employed full time. Predictors of work disability in panic patients include factors such as panic frequency, illness attitudes, and family dissatisfaction. Panic disorder patients were found to have mental health and role functioning competence substantially lower than those patients with other major chronic medical illnesses.

The severity and frequency of panic attacks vary widely. For example, one patient may experience a panic attack once a week for months at a time, while another may describe a string of attacks in a week, separated by periods of weeks to months for many years without attacks. Limited-symptom panic attacks (four or fewer symptoms of full panic-attack criteria) also are very common in patients with panic disorder. Patients also worry about the complications or consequences of the panic attacks. Some fear that it indicates that they have a life-threatening illness, such as myocardial infarction or seizures. Patients often present to an emergency room or internist for a medical work-up, which documents no acute medical problem. Others may feel that panic attacks are a sign that they are going crazy. Many patients with panic disorder also can develop avoidance behavior and agoraphobia (anxiety about being in places or situations from which escape might be difficult or embarrassing, or where help is not available).

A central factor in the pathophysiology of panic is hyperventilation. Patients with panic disorder have been shown to be chronic hyperventilators who also acutely hyperventilate spontaneously, inducing panic attacks. This hyperventilation then induces hypocapnia and alkalosis, leading to decreased cerebral blood flow and, subsequently, dizziness, confusion, and derealization. These signs and symptoms of hyperventilation are successfully treated with antipanic medications or with appropriate behavior breathing techniques, such as slow nasal and abdominal breathing exercises.

The lifetime prevalence of panic disorder with or without agoraphobia ranges from 1.5% to 3.5%, with 1-year prevalence rates between 1% and 2%. About half of patients with panic disorder have agoraphobia. The age of onset ranges between the late teens and the early to mid 30s, with a bimodal distribution. The course of panic disorder varies from episodic to chronic. The course and association of agoraphobia with panic disorder also vary from episodic to chronic. Women are more often affected than are men by a ratio of 2:1 to 3:1. Women also tend to have a greater incidence of panic disorder between 25 and 44 years of age, and their attacks tend to continue longer into older age. With treatment, about 30% of patients are well after 10 years, 40% to 50% are somewhat improved

Table 1: Differential Diagnoses of Panic Disorder

- Anxiety from a general medical condition, such as thyroid disease, parathyroid disease, cardiac arrhythmia, coronary artery disease, pheochromocytoma, hypoglycemia, vertigo, mitral valve prolapse
- Anxiety from substance use or withdrawal
- Social phobia (panic attacks situationally bound to social encounters and not unexpected)
- Specific phobia (panic attacks cued by a situation or object)
- Obsessive-compulsive disorder (panic attacks cued by exposure to the feared object of obsession)
- Posttraumatic stress disorder (panic attacks cued by stimuli related to the traumatic stressor)
- Depressive disorders
- Psychotic disorders such as schizophrenia
- Depersonalization disorder
- Somatoform disorders
- Personality disorders

but still symptomatic, and the remaining 20% to 30% remain unchanged or have become worse. Patients with panic disorder and agoraphobia tend to have lower remission rates (20% at 18 months follow-up) and higher relapse rates, compared with those without agoraphobia. The prognosis is also worse for patients with comorbid depression or personality disorders.

On physical examination, patients with panic disorder often have transient tachycardia and elevation of systolic blood pressure during some panic attacks. Some studies have shown an association between panic disorder and thyroid disease, mitral valve prolapse, vestibular problems, and asthma. Patients with panic disorder also have an increased death rate from cardiovascular illness, and a higher risk for the development of stroke. Significant psychiatric comorbidity also occurs in panic disorder. Major depressive disorder occurs in 50% to 60% of panic disorder patients. In about one third of these patients, the depressive disorder precedes the panic disorder. A subset of panic disorder patients also has comorbid substance-related disorders. These patients often self-medicate with alcohol, benzodiazepines, cannabis, cocaine, or other medications. Comorbidity with other anxiety disorders also is common, such as social phobia (15% to 30%), obsessive-compulsive disorder (8% to 10%), specific phobia (10% to 20%), and generalized anxiety disorder (25%). An increased suicide risk in uncomplicated panic disorder patients has also been found (7%), and this is substantially higher in panic disorder with comorbid psychiatric disorders. The differential diagnoses of panic disorder are outlined in Table 1.

Treatment

Treatment includes cognitive-behavior therapy and pharmacotherapy. In single-medication trials, the acute response rate is 50% to 60%. This rate increases with augmentation strategies. Acute treatment with medications includes tricyclic antidepressants (TCAs) such as imipramine, high-potency benzodiazepines such as alprazolam (Xanax®) and clonazepam (Klonopin®), monoamine oxidase inhibitors (MAOIs) such as phenelzine (Nardil®), and selective serotonin reuptake inhibitors (SSRIs) such as fluoxetine (Prozac®), paroxetine (Paxil®), sertraline (Zoloft®), and fluvoxamine (Luvox®).

The general principle for treatment of panic disorder is to reserve benzodiazepines until different antidepressants have been tried and have failed. It may also be necessary to acutely treat a patient with a benzodiazepine, and then switch the patient to an antidepressant. Full remission of panic attacks with antidepressants usually requires 4 to 12 weeks of treatment. Treatment usually is recommended for at least 6 months to prevent early relapse. However, acute treatment unfortunately does not usually lead to long-term remission. In a 1- to 4-year follow-up after acute imipramine treatment, 80% of patients were symptomatic. In a 3-year follow-up study with acute diazepam, alprazolam, or placebo, 60% showed continued symptoms. Therefore, maintenance treatment may be indicated for many panic patients. Physicians and patients should meet every several months to decrease the dose of medication, to eventually reach a minimum dose at which the patient remains symptom free.

Selected Readings

Allgulander C, Lavori PW: Excess mortality among 3302 patients with 'pure' anxiety neurosis. *Arch Gen Psychiatry* 1991;48: 599-602.

American Psychiatric Association: *Diagnostic and Statistical Manual of Mental Disorders*, 4th ed. Washington, DC, American Psychiatric Association, 1994.

Asmundson GJ, Larsen DK, Stein MB: Panic disorder and vestibular disturbance: an overview of empirical findings and clinical implications. *J Psychosom Res* 1998;44:107-120.

Ballenger JC, Burrows GD, DuPont RL Jr, et al: Alprazolam in panic disorder and agoraphobia: results from a multicenter trial. I. Efficacy in short-term treatment. *Arch Gen Psychiatry* 1988;45: 413-422.

Ballenger JC, Wheadon DE, Steiner M, et al: Double-blind, fixed-dose, placebo-controlled study of paroxetine in the treatment of panic disorder. *Am J Psychiatry* 1998;155:36-42.

Clark DM, Salkovskis PM, Chalkley AJ: Respiratory control as a treatment for panic attacks. *J Behav Ther Exp Psychiatry* 1985; 16:23-30.

Coryell W, Noyes R, Clancy J: Excess mortality in panic disorder. A comparison with primary unipolar depression. *Arch Gen Psychiatry* 1982;39:701-703.

de Boer JA: Serotonergic mechanisms in anxiety disorders: an inquiry into serotonin function in panic disorder. The Hague, Cip-Gegevens Koninklijke Bibliotheek, 1988.

Ettigi P, Meyerhoff AS, Chirban JT, et al: The quality of life and employment in panic disorder. *J Nerv Ment Dis* 1997;185:368-372.

Gunasekara NS, Noble S, Benfield P: Paroxetine. An update of its pharmacology and therapeutic use in depression and a review of its use in other disorders. *Drugs* 1998;55:85-120.

Hollander E, Simeon D, Gorman JM: Anxiety disorders. In: Hales RE, Yudofsky SC, Talbott JA, eds. *American Psychiatric Press Textbook of Psychiatry*, 2nd ed. Washington, DC, American Psychiatric Press, 1994.

Hollifield M, Katon W, Skipper B, et al: Panic disorder and quality of life: variables predictive of functional impairment. *Am J Psychiatry* 1997;154:766-772.

Johnson J, Weissman MM, Klerman GL: Panic disorder, comorbidity, and suicide attempts. *Arch Gen Psychiatry* 1990;47:805-808.

Katerndahl DA, Realini JP: Quality of life and panic-related work disability in subjects with infrequent panic and panic disorder. *J Clin Psychiatry* 1997;58:153-158.

Keller MB, Yonkers KA, Warshaw MG, et al: Remission and relapse in subjects with panic disorder and panic with agoraphobia: a prospective short-interval naturalistic follow-up. *J Nerv Ment Dis* 1994;182:290-296.

Klein DF: Delineation of two drug responsive anxiety syndromes. *Psychopharmacologia* 1964;5:397-408.

Lum LC: Hyperventilation and anxiety state. *J R Soc Med* 1981; 74:1-4.

McNair DM, Kahn RJ: Imipramine compared with a benzodiazepine for agoraphobia. In: Klein DF, Rabkin JG, eds. *Anxiety: New Research and Changing Concepts*. New York, Raven, 1981.

Noyes R Jr, Garvey MJ, Cook BL: Follow-up study of patients with panic disorder and agoraphobia with panic attacks treated with tricyclic antidepressants. *J Affect Disord* 1989;16:249-257.

Regier DA, Boyd JH, Burke JD Jr, et al: One-month prevalence of mental disorders in the United States. Based on five Epidemiologic Catchment Area sites. *Arch Gen Psychiatry* 1988; 45:977-986.

Rosenbaum JF, Moroz G, Bowden CL: Clonazepam in the treatment of panic disorder with or without agoraphobia: a dose-response study of efficacy, safety, and discontinuance. Clonazepam Panic Disorder Dose-Response Study Group. *J Clin Psychopharmacol* 1997;17:390-400.

Sheehan DV, Ballenger J, Jacobsen G: Treatment of endogenous anxiety with phobic, hysterical, and hypochondriacal symptoms. *Arch Gen Psychiatry* 1980;37:51-59.

Sherbourne CD, Wells KB, Judd LL: Functioning and well-being of patients with panic disorder. *Am J Psychiatry* 1996;153: 213-218.

Smoller JW, Otto MW: Panic, dyspnea, and asthma. *Curr Opin Pulm Med* 1998;4:40-45.

Weissman MM, Markowitz JS, Ouellette R, et al: Panic disorder and cardiovascular/cerebrovascular problems: results from a community survey. *Am J Psychiatry* 1990;147:1504-1508.

Zitrin CM, Klein DF, Woerner MG: Treatment of agoraphobia with group exposure in vivo and imipramine. *Arch Gen Psychiatry* 1980;37:63-72.

Chapter **12**

Social Phobia

A patient's central fear in social phobia, or social anxiety disorder, is of acting in a way that might humiliate or embarrass oneself in front of others. Social phobic individuals fear and avoid situations that would require them to interact with others, or to perform a task such as speaking in front of others. Besides speaking, typical social fears include eating or writing in public, attending parties, being interviewed, or using public lavatories. An individual may have one or many social fears. Exposure to the feared situation provokes anxiety, which may manifest as a situationally provoked panic attack accompanied by blushing, sweating, and dry mouth. In contrast, panic disorder patients tend to have palpitations and chest pain. In children, social anxiety may be expressed by crying, tantrums, freezing up, or shrinking from social situations with unfamiliar people. Adult and adolescent sufferers often recognize that the fear is excessive or unreasonable. Social phobics often use alcohol and sedatives as self-medication for the anxiety symptoms, a behavior that can lead to abuse. Patients with generalized social phobia tend to be younger, less educated, and have greater anxiety and depression than patients with public-speaking social phobia.

Common personality features of patients with social phobia include hypersensitivity to criticism, negative evaluation, or rejection; difficulty being assertive; and low self-esteem. Patients may also be socially awkward (eg, have difficulty making eye contact) or have observable signs of anxiety such as clammy hands, tremors, or a shaky voice. Social phobics often underachieve in school and at work because of the anxiety or avoidance behavior, and their social lives are often affected, leading to significant educational and economic incapacitation. One study found that up to 20% of social phobics are on welfare.

The lifetime prevalence rate of social phobia ranges from 3% to 13%, affecting more women than men. Comorbid diagnoses include simple phobia, panic disorder, agoraphobia, obsessive-compulsive disorder, mood disorders such as major depression and dysthymia, substance-related disorders, somatization disorder, and avoidant personality disorder. Studies indicate that social phobics with additional comorbid Axis I diagnoses are more depressed and anxious than those without. Patients with comorbid Axis II disorders are more depressed but not more anxious than those without. These individuals rarely present for inpatient treatment of social phobia, the onset of which often occurs in the teenage years, although some in early childhood. Onset may occur abruptly after a stressful or humiliating experience, or may be gradual. Duration is often lifelong with a continuous course.

Case Report

TS was a 20-year-old, single, white, female college student who had been having problems with avoidance, anxiety, and not wanting to go out. Her parents decided she needed to be evaluated. On presentation, she reported that she had problems being around other people, fearing that they would say something bad about her. She would get nervous and tongue-tied. As a result, she rarely went out for fear of being humiliated in public. She also had situational panic attacks in crowds, and soon started getting depressed because she 'had no life' and her schoolwork

Table 1: Differential Diagnoses of Panic Disorder

- Panic disorder with agoraphobia, in which the panic attacks are not limited to social situations

- Generalized anxiety disorder, in which the fear of humiliation is not the main focus of fear and anxiety

- Schizoid personality disorder, in which social situations are avoided because of a lack of interest in relating to others

- Mood disorders such as major depression and dysthymia, in which social anxiety and withdrawal are common features but are secondary to the depressive syndrome

- Body dysmorphic disorder, in which avoidance is secondary to fear of rejection from the perceived body defect

- Psychotic disorders, in which avoidance of social situations may be attributable to paranoia

- Avoidant personality disorder, which develops in childhood and often follows early childhood shyness and social phobia

- Performance anxiety, stage fright, and shyness, which do not lead to clinically significant impairment, but may represent a subtype of (discrete) social phobia

was being affected. She could not understand what was wrong with her and felt that she must be 'weird' in some way. She lost many friends and became virtually homebound except for going to classes, which she would also avoid doing when she could. She was treated with paroxetine (Paxil®) 20 mg/d, which helped the anxiety and avoidance symptoms. She also began cognitive-behavior therapy, and her parents received psychoeducation. She is now doing well in school, received a much-coveted summer internship at a New York fashion house, reinstituted old friendships, and is no longer depressed.

The differential diagnoses of social phobia are listed in Table 1.

Treatment

Both pharmacologic treatment with selective serotonin reuptake inhibitors (SSRIs) or with monoamine oxidase inhibitors (MAOIs), and cognitive-behavior treatments (eg, cognitive restructuring, in vivo exposure, and social skills training) have been found to be effective in the treatment of social phobia. In fact, the two treatments often appear to complement each other. Pharmacologic treatment can be selected by social phobia subtype. In performance-type social phobia, treatment with beta-blockers before the social event may be helpful; for example, 10 to 20 mg of propranolol (Inderal®) orally 1 hour before the event. The patient should test the effect of the beta-blockers before the event to evaluate effectiveness and emergence of any side effects.

The use of MAOIs, such as phenelzine (Nardil®), has been found to be highly effective in mixed social phobia-agoraphobia subpopulations. For example, two thirds of patients responded to 45 to 90 mg/d of phenelzine compared to atenolol (Tenormin®), which had no effect on symptoms. In addition, tranylcypromine (Parnate®) in dosages of 40 to 60 mg/d improved symptoms in about 80% of patients treated openly for 1 year. However, because of potential side effects, such as the rare hypertensive crisis, MAOIs are not a first-line treatment for social phobia. Moclobemide, a reversible inhibitor of MAOI that is safer than the nonreversible MAOIs, was also found to be more effective than placebo, but is not available in the United States.

SSRIs have also been shown to be effective in the treatment of social phobia, and are the first-line treatment of choice. A double-blind, placebo-controlled trial with fluvoxamine (Luvox®) in doses of 150 mg/d has proven helpful in social phobics. Fluoxetine (Prozac®) has been found to be effective, with starting doses of 20 mg and flexible titration. Paroxetine has been found to be effective in treating generalized social phobia with starting doses of 10 mg/d and titration dependent on clinical response and side effects. Paroxetine has received a specific FDA indication for social phobia. Some patients may also respond to atypical antidepressants such as nefazodone (Serzone®).

Buspirone (BuSpar®) was not found to be effective in treating social phobia when used alone, but has been proven useful when used to augment an SSRI. Venlafaxine (Effexor®), a serotonin-norepinephrine reuptake inhibitor, also decreased social phobia symptoms in a small open trial in which patients were treated with smaller doses than those recommended for the treatment of depression. Benzodiazepines such as alprazolam (Xanax®) or clonazepam (Klonopin®) can also be used in the short term if appropriate, but they are not recommended for long-term maintenance treatment because of the potential for abuse, rebound, and withdrawal symptoms.

Selected Readings

American Psychiatric Association: *Diagnostic and Statistical Manual of Mental Disorders*, 4th ed. Washington, DC, American Psychiatric Association, 1994.

Fones CS, Manfro GG, Pollack MH: Social phobia: an update. *Harv Rev Psychiatry* 1998;5:247-259.

Gottschalk LA, Stone MN, Gleser CG: Peripheral versus central mechanisms accounting for antianxiety effects of propranolol. *Psychosom Med* 1974;36:47-56.

Hartley LR, Ungapen S, Davie I, et al: The effect of beta adrenergic blocking drugs on speakers' performance and memory. *Br J Psychiatry* 1983;142:512-517.

Heimberg RG, Hope DA, Dodge CS, et al: DSM-III-R subtypes of social phobia: comparison of generalized social phobics and public speaking phobics. *J Nerv Ment Dis* 1990;178:172-179.

Hollander E, Simeon D, Gorman JM: Anxiety disorders. In: Hales RE, Yudofsky SC, Talbott JA, eds. *American Psychiatric Press Textbook of Psychiatry*, 2nd ed. Washington DC, American Psychiatric Press, 1994.

Kelsey JE: Venlafaxine in social phobia. *Psychopharmacol Bull* 1995;31:767-771.

Lepine JP, Lellouch J: Classification and epidemiology of social phobia. *Eur Arch Psychiatry Clin Neurosci* 1995;244:290-296.

Liebowitz MR, Schneier F, Campeas R, et al: Phenelzine vs atenolol in social phobia. A placebo-controlled comparison. *Arch Gen Psychiatry* 1992;49:290-300.

Mancini C, Ameringen MV: Paroxetine in social phobia. *J Clin Psychiatry* 1996;57:519-522.

Rapaport MH, Paniccia G, Judd LL: A review of social phobia. *Psychopharmacol Bull* 1995;31:125-129.

Reich DA, Noyes R, Yates W: Anxiety symptoms distinguishing social phobia from panic and generalized anxiety disorders. *Am J Psychiatry* 1989;146:513-516.

Schneier FR, Goetz D, Campeas R, et al: Placebo-controlled trial of moclobemide in social phobia. *Br J Psychiatry* 1998;172:70-77.

Schneier FR, Saoud JB, Campeas R, et al: Buspirone in social phobia. *J Clin Psychopharmacol* 1993;13:251-256.

Turner SM, Beidel DC, Borden JW, et al: Social phobia: Axis I and II correlates. *J Abnorm Psychol* 1991;100:102-106.

Van Ameringen M, Mancini C, Streiner DL: Fluoxetine efficacy in social phobia. *J Clin Psychiatry* 1993;54:27-32.

Van Ameringen M, Mancini C, Streiner D: Sertraline in social phobia. *J Affect Disord* 1994;31:141-145.

Van Ameringen M, Mancini C, Wilson C: Buspirone augmentation of selective serotonin reuptake inhibitors (SSRIs) in social phobia. *J Affect Disord* 1996;39:115-121.

van Vliet IM, den Boer JA, Westenberg HG: Psychopharmacological treatment of social phobia: a double blind placebo controlled study with fluvoxamine. *Psychopharmacology (Berl)* 1994;115: 128-134.

van Vliet IM, den Boer JA, Westenberg HG, et al: Clinical effects of buspirone in social phobia: a double-blind placebo-controlled study. *J Clin Psychiatry* 1997;58:164-168.

Versiani M, Mundim FD, Nardi AE, et al: Tranylcypromine in social phobia. *J Clin Psychopharmacol* 1988;8:279-283.

Chapter **13**

Obsessive-Compulsive Disorders

Obsessive-compulsive disorders (OCD) are characterized by recurrent obsessions and compulsions that cause marked distress and significant functional impairment. Obsessive-compulsive spectrum disorders, which are addressed in Chapter 14, are a group of disorders with overlapping symptoms and compulsive qualities, and preferential response to serotonin reuptake inhibitors (SRIs) and to cognitive-behavior therapy, but are otherwise distinct disorders from OCD. Both patients and their families are substantially affected. In addition, the economic consequences of OCD are great. One study has estimated that the direct costs for OCD treatment in the United States is about $5 billion a year. More disturbingly, the cost per patient for ineffective treatments because of *misdiagnosis* is significantly higher than that for specific, appropriate, and effective treatment.

Clinicians should understand the importance of distinguishing true obsessions from obsessive brooding, ruminations, or preoccupations that are not ego-dystonic. They should also distinguish true compulsions from other activities that are typically called compulsive, such as excessive eating, drinking, and sexual behavior, which are experienced as pleasurable, although their consequences can often be unpleasant. Anxiety is often associated with obsessions and resistance to compulsions. In addition, the anxiety is often immediately relieved by yielding to the compulsions. Although most OCD patients acknowledge that their behavior is excessive, a subpopulation of patients lack any insight and are convinced that their obsessions and compulsions are reasonable.

Examples of common obsessions include preoccupation with dirt, germs, and contamination; fears about harming oneself or others because of past misdeeds or failure to carry out a ritual; religious obsessions; and sexual and aggressive imagery such as murder and rape.

Common compulsions include excessive hand-washing in 25% to 50% of OCD patients, checking behavior associated with pathologic doubt (ie, compulsively checking a lock or faucet), and mental compulsions such as repeating and replaying things repetitively in one's mind, or counting incessantly. OCD patients also frequently avoid situations that involve the content of their obsessions, such as avoiding public bathrooms for fear of feces or germs.

Associated findings in an OCD subpopulation include the presence of neurologic signs, such as motor coordination problems (associated with more severe disease), and the development of comorbid anxiety and depressive disorder. Neuropsychiatric findings in OCD patients include frontal lobe deficits and visual/spatial and constructional impairments.

Symptom cluster subtypes found in OCD include:
- patients obsessed with dirt and contamination whose rituals center on washing and cleaning, and tend not to be tic-related;
- patients obsessed with symmetry whose rituals center on arranging and rearranging things to be orderly and symmetric; affects more males than females; patients tend to have a positive family history and longer duration of illness;
- patients with OCD defined as the early-onset group that usually is tic-associated and affects more males than females who count and check compulsively;

- purely 'obsessional' patients with no compulsions;
- patients with primary obsessional slowness, who may take hours to complete any task;
- patients who compulsively hoard nonuseful material such as old newspapers and mail;
- patients with PANDAS (pediatric autoimmune neuro-psychiatric disorders associated with streptococcal infections), who usually have an abrupt onset of OCD symptoms in childhood after infection with group A beta-hemolytic streptococci; they tend to have a positive D8/17 B-cell marker also found in rheumatic fever.

The lifetime prevalence rate in OCD is as high as 3%, with a 6-month prevalence as high as 2%. These numbers may underestimate the actual incidence because of underreporting and the secretive nature of patients with this disorder. On the other hand, the numbers may be overestimated because the instruments used in community surveys may overdiagnose the true incidence. OCD affects males and females equally in adulthood, but males have an earlier age of onset (ages 6 to 15 years) compared to females (ages 20 to 29 years). Most patients experience a waxing and waning course, with about 15% experiencing a slow deterioration and another 5% having an episodic course.

Case Report

EF was a 36-year-old, single, unemployed female, with a community college degree, living with her mother. She was referred for treatment of obsessive-compulsive disorder. Her symptoms began when she was 16 years old with intrusive, unwanted thoughts and obsessions about violent acts, such as killing a cat or jumping in front of a train. These obsessive thoughts became so persistent that they took up all her free time and significantly interfered with her schooling.

She then developed obsessions and compulsions around the number 13 (tapping rituals, counting, undoing). She finally sought help when she was 21 because she felt "over-

Table 1: Comorbid Disorders Commonly Found in OCD Patients

- Depressive disorders that affect females more than males with OCD; up to two thirds of OCD patients have a lifetime comorbid depression

- Eating disorders such as anorexia nervosa, which affect more women than men

- Tourette's syndrome, which occurs in 5% to 7% of OCD patients; in fact, 35% to 50% of Tourette's patients have OCD

- Tics, past or current, in 20% to 30% of patients; tics are more common in male than in female patients

- Alcohol and substance abuse, which are more common in male OCD patients than in females

- Body dysmorphic disorder, which was found in up to one third of OCD patients sampled in the DSM-IV field trial

- Other anxiety disorders such as panic disorder and social phobia

- Psychotic disorders such as schizophrenia

whelmed and scattered" with depressive thoughts. On occasion she actually nearly stabbed the cat, and eventually hung it out the window. She was treated only with psychotherapy at that time. At age 28, she was referred to a psychiatrist who diagnosed her with OCD and treated her with fluoxetine (Prozac®), up to 80 mg/d but without improvement. She was then put on different medications, including thioridazine (Mellaril®), lithium (Lithobid®), clomipramine (Anafranil®), and combinations of fluoxetine and pimozide (Orap®), and fluoxetine and clomipramine, which helped

Table 2: Differential Diagnoses of OCD

- Psychotic disorders, such as schizophrenia and delusional disorder, in which delusions must be distinguished from obsessions

- Depression, especially psychotic and agitated depressions, with patients tending to have significant obsessional symptoms, including ego-dystonic morbid ruminations

- Phobic disorders

- Body dysmorphic disorder, in which preoccupations and rituals are specifically related to the person's appearance

- Hypochondriasis, in which the distressing thoughts are solely related to having a serious disease

- Obsessive-compulsive personality disorder, which involves a pervasive pattern of preoccupation with orderliness, perfectionism and control, and where patients are stubborn, stingy, bogged down in detail, and seriously distract coworkers and spouses, but do not experience obsessions and compulsions

only partially. She was finally hospitalized at age 32 with symptoms of major depression in addition to the OCD. She did not have any psychotic symptoms at that time. She had tried cognitive-behavior treatment but was too anxious to tolerate it. She was finally discharged on a combination of clomipramine, valproate (Depakote®), and clonazepam (Klonopin®), and has been fairly stable since.

Comorbidity with other psychiatric and neurologic illnesses is common in OCD. The morbidity risk was found to be about 5.4% in some studies. Patients with OCD and other comorbid psychiatric disorders have a significantly elevated risk of suicide. The comorbid disorders common in OCD patients are listed in Table 1.

Table 2 lists the differential diagnoses of OCD.

Treatment

OCD has been found to respond to selective serotonin reuptake inhibitors (SSRIs) and behavior therapy (exposure/response prevention), and perhaps best to a combination of these two treatments. However, some patients may not be able to tolerate behavior therapy because of intense anxiety and comorbid conditions such as depression or poor insight, or because well-trained behavior therapists are not available. These patients should be medicated adequately before again trying behavior therapy. An adequate duration for a pharmacologic trial is at least 12 weeks at the maximum tolerated dose. However, improvement of symptoms can be relatively slow and can take weeks, so patients must be forewarned that they may experience side effects before they notice any therapeutic effects of the medication. Treatment should be continued for at least 1 year after establishing a regimen that works. OCD patients tend to require much higher doses of medications compared to those used to treat depression.

The first medication studied in OCD was clomipramine. On a dose of 200 to 250 mg/d, the average reduction in OC symptoms was 40%, and about 60% of patients were clinically much or very much improved. The SSRIs fluoxetine, fluvoxamine (Luvox®), sertraline (Zoloft®), and paroxetine (Paxil®) have been shown to be effective in the treatment of OCD in 43% to 71% of patients, and have established indications by the FDA for OCD.

For patients who do not respond to the first SSRI agent used, switching to a different SSRI should be tried because 25% of patients who have failed one may respond

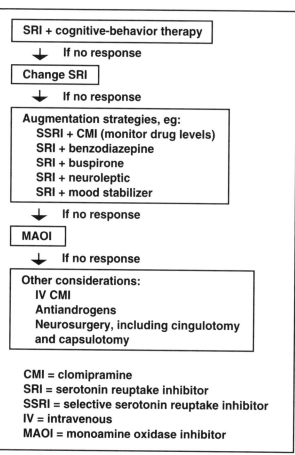

SRI + cognitive-behavior therapy

↓ If no response

Change SRI

↓ If no response

Augmentation strategies, eg:
    SSRI + CMI (monitor drug levels)
    SRI + benzodiazepine
    SRI + buspirone
    SRI + neuroleptic
    SRI + mood stabilizer

↓ If no response

MAOI

↓ If no response

Other considerations:
    IV CMI
    Antiandrogens
    Neurosurgery, including cingulotomy
    and capsulotomy

CMI = clomipramine
SRI = serotonin reuptake inhibitor
SSRI = selective serotonin reuptake inhibitor
IV = intravenous
MAOI = monoamine oxidase inhibitor

Figure 1: A treatment algorithm for OCD. A therapeutic trial for any medication or combination of medications is 12 weeks. If treatment is successful, continue treatment for at least 12 months.

to another. Augmentation strategies can also be used based on the patient's primary symptom cluster and comorbidity profile. These are examined in Chapter 16 (*Refractory*

Anxiety). Other more novel approaches include the use of MAOIs, inositol, repetitive transcranial magnetic stimulation, intravenous clomipramine, and antiandrogens. Figure 1 is a treatment algorithm for OCD.

Selected Readings

American Psychiatric Association: *Diagnostic and Statistical Manual of Mental Disorders,* 4th ed. Washington, DC, American Psychiatric Association, 1994.

Aronowitz BR, Hollander E, DeCaria CM, et al: Neuropsychology of obsessive-compulsive disorder. Preliminary findings. *Neuropsychiatry Neuropsychol Behav Neurol* 1994;7:81-86.

Castle DJ, Deale A, Marks IM: Gender differences in obsessive compulsive disorder. *Aust N Z J Psychiatry* 1995;29:114-117.

Flament MF, Rapoport JL, Berg CJ, et al: Clomipramine treatment of childhood obsessive-compulsive disorder. A double-blind controlled study. *Arch Gen Psychiatry* 1985;42:977-983.

Goodman WK, Price LH, Rasmussen SA, et al: Efficacy of fluvoxamine in obsessive-compulsive disorder. A double-blind comparison with placebo. *Arch Gen Psychiatry* 1989;46:36-44.

Greist J, Chouinard G, DuBoff E, et al: Double-blind parallel comparison of three dosages of sertraline and placebo in outpatients with obsessive-compulsive disorder. *Arch Gen Psychiatry* 1995;52:289-295.

Hantouche EG, Lancrenon S: Modern typology of symptoms and obsessive-compulsive syndromes: results of a large French study of 615 patients. *Encephale* 1996;22:9-21.

Head D, Bolton D, Hymas N: Deficit in cognitive shifting ability in patients with obsessive-compulsive disorder. *Biol Psychiatry* 1989;25:929-937.

Hollander E, DeCaria CM, Aronowitz B, et al: A pilot follow-up study of childhood soft signs and the development of adult psychopathology. *J Neuropsychiatry Clin Neurosci* 1991;3:186-189.

Hollander E, Greenwald S, Neville D, et al: Uncomplicated and comorbid obsessive-compulsive disorder in an epidemiologic sample. *Depress Anxiety* 1996;4:111-119.

Hollander E, Simeon D, Gorman JM: Anxiety disorders. In: Hales RE, Yudofsky SC, Talbott JA, eds. *American Psychiatric Press*

Textbook of Psychiatry, 2nd ed. Washington, DC, American Psychiatric Press, 1994.

Hollander E, Stein DJ, Kwon JH, et al: Psychosocial function and economic costs of obsessive-compulsive disorder. *CNS Spectrums* 1997;2:16-25.

Hollander E, Wong CM: Body dysmorphic disorder, pathological gambling, and sexual compulsions. *J Clin Psychiatry* 1995;56:7-12.

Holzer JC, Goodman WK, McDougle DJ, et al: Obsessive-compulsive disorder with and without a chronic tic disorder. A comparison of symptoms in 70 patients. *Br J Psychiatry* 1994;164:469-473.

Insel TR, Donnelly ER, Lalakea ML, et al: Neurological and neuropsychological studies of patients with obsessive-compulsive disorder. *Biol Psychiatry* 1983;18:741-751.

Jenike MA, Baer L, Minichiello WE, et al: Placebo-controlled trial of fluoxetine and phenelzine for obsessive-compulsive disorder. *Am J Psychiatry* 1997;154:1261-1264.

Kaye NS, Dancu C: Paroxetine and obsessive-compulsive disorder. *Am J Psychiatry* 1994;151:1523.

Kolada JL, Bland RC, Newman SC: Epidemiology of psychiatric disorders in Edmonton. Obsessive-compulsive disorder. *Acta Psychiatr Scand Suppl* 1994;376:24-35.

Kozak MJ, Foa EB: Obsessions, overvalued ideas, and delusions in obsessive-compulsive-disorder. *Behav Res Ther* 1994;32:343-353.

Myers JK, Weissman MM, Tischler GL, et al: Six-month prevalence of psychiatric disorders in three communities 1980 to 1982. *Arch Gen Psychiatry* 1984;41:959-967.

Nicolini H, Weissbecker K, Mejia JM, et al: Family study of obsessive-compulsive disorder in a Mexican population. *Arch Med Res* 1993;24:193-198.

Noshirvani HF, Kasvikis Y, Marks IM, et al: Gender-divergent aetiological factors in obsessive-compulsive disorder. *Br J Psychiatry* 1991;258:260-263.

Pauls DL, Alsobrook JP 2nd, Goodman W, et al: A family study of obsessive-compulsive disorder. *Am J Psychiatry* 1995;152:76-84.

Pitman RK, Green RC, Jenike MA, et al: Clinical comparison of Tourette's disorder and obsessive-compulsive disorder. *Am J Psychiatry* 1987;144:1166-1171.

Rachman SJ, Hodgson RJ: *Obsessions and Compulsions.* Englewood Cliffs, NJ, Prentice-Hall, 1980.

Rasmussen SA, Tsuang MT: Clinical characteristics and family history in DSM-III obsessive-compulsive disorder. *Am J Psychiatry* 1986;143:317-322.

Rasmussen SA, Tsuang MT: The epidemiology of obsessive compulsive disorder. *J Clin Psychiatry* 1984;45:450-457.

Robins LN, Helzer JE, Weissman MM, et al: Lifetime prevalence of specific psychiatric disorders in three sites. *Arch Gen Psychiatry* 1984;41:949-958.

Simeon D, Hollander E, Stein DJ, et al: Body dysmorphic disorder in the DSM-IV field trial for obsessive-compulsive disorder. *Am J Psychiatry* 1995;152:1207-1209.

Swedo SE, Leonard HL, Mittleman BB, et al: Identification of children with pediatric autoimmune neuropsychiatric disorders associated with streptococcal infections by a marker associated with rheumatic fever. *Am J Psychiatry* 1997;154:110-112.

Thomsen PH: Obsessive-compulsive disorder in children and adolescents. A 6-22 year follow-up study of social outcome. *Eur Child Adolesc Psychiatry* 1995;4:112-122.

Tollefson GD, Rampey AH Jr, Potvin JH, et al: A multicenter investigation of fixed-dose fluoxetine in the treatment of obsessive-compulsive disorder. *Arch Gen Psychiatry* 1994;51:559-567.

Zohar AH, Ratsoni G, Pauls DL, et al: An epidemiological study of obsessive-compulsive disorder and related disorders in Israeli adolescents. *J Am Acad Child Adolesc Psychiatry* 1992;31:1057-1061.

Chapter **14**

Obsessive-Compulsive Spectrum Disorders

C linicians have recently emphasized the relationship between obsessive-compulsive disorder (OCD) and related or spectrum disorders. The obsessive-compulsive spectrum disorders may conceivably affect up to 10% of the United States population. This chapter defines and elucidates the OCD spectrum and focuses on treatment issues.

OC spectrum disorders (Table 1), which have overlapping symptoms and compulsive qualities with OCD, but are distinct disorders, include many distinct psychiatric categories. The *somatoform disorders group* is marked by a preoccupation with bodily appearance or sensations, with compulsive behaviors performed to decrease anxiety brought on by these preoccupations. These disorders include hypochondriasis and body dysmorphic disorder (BDD), both characterized by a preoccupation with bodily features. In hypochondriasis, persons are obsessed or preoccupied with having some kind of physical illness in the absence of confirmatory medical evidence. In BDD, the patient is preoccupied with an imagined flaw in appearance in some part of the body. Patients with these disorders may have a fixity of beliefs, contributing to the treatment resistance in BDD, hypochondriasis, and anorexia nervosa.

The *eating disorder group* of OC spectrum disorders includes anorexia nervosa, bulimia, and binge eating. Per-

Table 1: Obsessive-Compulsive Spectrum Disorders

Somatoform disorders

- hypochondriasis
- body dysmorphic disorder

Eating disorders

- anorexia nervosa
- bulimia
- binge eating

Impulse control disorders

- pathologic gambling
- trichotillomania
- kleptomania
- compulsive buying
- nail-biting
- sexual compulsions
- self-injurious behavior

Neurologic cluster disorders

- Sydenham's chorea
- autism and Asperger's syndrome
- Tourette's syndrome

Delusional cluster disorders

- obsessional jealousy
- comorbid schizotypal personality
- schizophrenic patients with comorbid OC symptoms

Stereotypic movement disorders

- head-banging
- onychophagia
- skin-picking

sons with anorexia nervosa have an average of 10 obsessive-compulsive concerns that are unrelated to their characteristic obsessions about body weight, body image, diet, exercise, or food preparation. Anorexic patients may become more obsessional when they are starving, but after they recover their weight, they continue to exhibit other obsessive-compulsive traits. Eating-disorder patients may develop serious medical problems if their disorder is untreated. Co-treatment by an internist is helpful in such cases to devise a comprehensive treatment plan to deal with the medical complications.

The *neurologic cluster* may include Sydenham's chorea, autism and Asperger's syndrome, and Tourette's syndrome. The neurologic cluster involves little obsessional content and mostly manifests motoric, repetitive symptoms. It resembles the 'just-so,' symmetric subtype of OCD addressed in Chapter 13.

Autism affects social, communicative, and imaginative development, with a compulsive core characterized by stereotypic movements, craving for sameness, and narrow repetitive interests. Asperger's syndrome involves less severe speech disturbance than autism, but still affects social development with associated stereotypies and narrow repetitive interests. Tourette's syndrome comprises multiple motor and vocal tics with associated obsessions and compulsions. Sydenham's chorea occurs secondary to rheumatic fever, involves the basal ganglia, and has associated repetitive involuntary movements and anxiety.

Basal ganglia involvement in these disorders often gives rise to the development of stereotypic movements. These disorders often have a compulsive core, but the nature of the obsessions and compulsions experienced by these patients is often qualitatively different from that experienced by patients with OCD per se. For example, in autism, McDougle et al found less preoccupation with aggressiveness, counting, sexual and religious matter, symmetry, and somatic obsessions. Autism does, however, involve a relative increase in repetition and ordering, hoarding, telling or asking, touching, tapping, and self-mutilation behavior. In patients with tic disorders, touching, tapping, rubbing, blinking, and staring rituals appear more prominent, with fewer cleaning rituals. In Tourette's syndrome, sensory phenomena often precede intentional repetitive behaviors, whereas in OCD, the behaviors are usually preceded by cognitions and autonomic anxiety instead.

Impulse control disorders include pathologic gambling, trichotillomania, kleptomania, compulsive buying, nail-biting, sexual compulsions, and self-injurious behavior. Impulse control disorders are characterized by failure to resist impulses with harmful consequences, increasing tension or arousal before the act, pleasure, gratification or release during the act, and possible feelings of regret or guilt afterwards. These disorders are difficult to treat because many patients favor the associated 'high' that these behaviors give them. Some clinicians would consider these disorders as forms of addiction and would advocate that these patients also need additional motivational therapy to help engage and keep them in treatment, such as Gamblers Anonymous and similar support groups.

Impulsive behavior has no clear functional significance with regard to anxiety regulation (either increased or decreased), but the purpose of the behaviors appears to center on pleasure regulation. The largest obstacle to treating these patients is keeping them engaged in therapy. Insufficient or inadequate treatment secondary to poor follow-up often leads to a resurgence of symptoms and illness relapse.

The *delusional cluster* of patients in the OC spectrum includes those with somatic and jealous subtypes of delusional disorder, with associated obsessions and compulsions related to their delusions. These patients generally have poorer treatment outcomes and tend to respond better to a combination of an SSRI and a dopamine-blocking agent. In addition to OCD patients with delusional conviction, OCD patients with comorbid schizotypal personality, and schizophrenic patients with comorbid OC symptoms, may be included in this category. Up to one quarter of schizophrenic patients may have substantial obsessive or compulsive symptoms, and aggressive treatment of these symptoms, in addition to treatment for psychosis, may substantially improve their long-term course.

The *stereotypic movement disorders* that fall within the OC spectrum are head-banging, onychophagia, and skin-picking. These patients compulsively exhibit associated movements that often result in some kind of trauma to their bodies. The dopaminergic (D_1 and D_2, in particular) and serotonergic systems have been shown to be involved in the production of stereotypies. The roles of the opiate system, other neuropeptides such as cholecystokinin and GABA, and the chloride and calcium-channel systems, have also been raised. Some patients with stereotypic movement disorders also have comorbid mental retardation. These patients tend to be less responsive to therapy.

It is important to note, however, that spectrum disorders often coexist in the same patient. Many patients with comorbid spectrum disorders are labeled as treatment resistant when they do not respond to conventional treatments that are targeted to a narrow diagnostic category. Therefore, knowledge of a broader spectrum of diagnostic entities that are often associated and interrelated would lead to more tailored treatments, and hopefully to improved response rates.

OC spectrum disorders share many features with OCD.
1. *Symptom Profile and Phenomenology*

OCD is characterized by either obsessions (recurrent and persistent ideas, thoughts, or images), or compulsions (repetitive behaviors performed according to certain rules or in a stereotyped fashion). In addition, these obsessions or compulsions cause marked distress or significantly interfere with the patient's function. Symptomatically, both compulsivity and impulsivity have in common the inability to inhibit or delay repetitive behaviors. The difference between the two lies in the driving foci. In compulsivity, the driving focus is the need to decrease the discomfort associated with rituals; in impulsivity, the driving focus is the need to maximize pleasure. However, not all compulsions reduce anxiety. In impulsive patients, an additional component of the rituals is pleasure, albeit with associated guilt after the behavior is carried out. Patients with OC-related disorders can manifest features of both compulsivity and impulsivity. Clearly, compulsivity and impulsivity are not mutually exclusive, and individuals may have one set of behaviors driven by the need to reduce anxiety, and another set of behaviors driven by the need to obtain pleasure. These disorders could be caused by differential dysregulation of 5-HT pathways in different brain areas, but more research needs to be done to investigate this possibility.

2. Associated Features

Although OCD can start as early as age 2, an increased incidence occurs in the teenage and early adult years. Likewise, the onset of OC spectrum disorders tends to be in adolescence or the early 20s. There is a higher incidence of positive family history of OCD, of other OC spectrum disorders, and of mood disorders. Also, comorbidity often occurs with other OC spectrum disorders.

Ego-dystonic features are more common in later-onset OCD cases compared with earlier-onset cases. Most cases seem to be chronic. Although there is no reported male or female preponderance in adult OCD, the spectrum disorders may differ with respect to gender. Females tend to be overrepresented in studies of body dysmorphic disorder, compulsive buying, and kleptomania. Males seem to predominate in pathologic gambling and hypochondriasis. It is not clear whether the differences are generated by endocrine, neuroanatomic, or social/cultural factors. In the subtypes of childhood-onset and tic-related OCD, up to 75% of patients are male.

3. Neurobiology

Neurobiologic models of OCD and spectrum disorders emphasize the role of serotonin (5-HT) in pathophysiologic mechanisms. In some studies of OCD, pharmacologic treatment with oral m-chlorophenylpiperazine (m-CPP), a partial serotonergic agonist, increased the severity of OC symptoms in a subgroup of OCD patients. To contrast with the impulsive end of the spectrum, borderline personality disorder patients with impulsive features were also studied using m-CPP. Instead of producing obsessional symptoms, disinhibition, or depersonalization, core symptoms of borderline personality disorder were instead produced. These studies point to differential dysregulation in 5-HT pathways in more compulsive versus more impulsive disorders. The differential dysregulation is significant because it may explain differences in response to SSRI treatment, such as lag of effective response and persistence of therapeutic response to SSRIs. Further studies are needed to address these findings to elucidate the pathophysiology of the various OC spectrum disorders and treatment implications.

4. Treatment Response

OCD and spectrum disorders appear to be preferentially responsive to treatment with the selective serotonin reuptake inhibitors (SSRIs) and with behavior therapy. Up to 60% of patients with OCD showed significant improvement during treatment with SSRIs, and this appears to be a selective efficacy to SSRIs. Norepinephrine reuptake inhibitors, such as desipramine (Norpramin®) and nortriptyline (Pamelor®), are ineffective. Response rates in some, but not all, studies have also been shown to increase to 90% with augmentation therapy with other serotonergic agents, such as buspirone (BuSpar®) and fenfluramine (Pondimin®) (which is no longer available in the United States), dopaminergic agents such as haloperidol (Haldol®), pimozide (Orap®), risperidone (Risperdal®), or GABA-ergic agents such as clonazepam (Klonopin®).

However, for the most part, double-blind, controlled trials of augmentation treatments are lacking. In addition, OC spectrum disorders are often comorbid, and misdiagnosis is frequent, leading to poor treatment response, as well as to true treatment resistance.

Treatment studies for the OC spectrum disorders have mostly been open clinical trials and are less well characterized than those for OCD. They have, however, shown preferential response to SSRIs for disorders such as BDD, hypochondriasis, depersonalization disorder, anorexia nervosa, pathologic gambling, sexual compulsions and paraphilias, self-injurious behavior, and trichotillomania. These studies indicate that subtle differential responses apparently exist between the impulsive and compulsive disorders with regard to dosage, response lag time, and maintenance of symptom remission. Patients with compulsive spectrum disorders, such as BDD and anorexia nervosa, have a significant lag time before response to SSRIs, but once they respond, they tend to maintain their gains as long as patients continue their treatment. Therefore, it is important to allow for an adequate trial at high enough doses before a patient is called a nonresponder or a partial responder.

On the other hand, patients with impulsive disorders, such as binge eating disorder and compulsive buying, often have a quick response to SSRIs that may diminish over time with treatment. These patients would therefore require addition of another agent after initial stabilization, such as a mood stabilizer.

Behavior therapy is also a mainstay of treatment in OCD and obsessive-compulsive spectrum disorders. Many of these patients benefit from prolonged exposure to feared situations (which is anxiety-provoking) and response prevention (which blocks the rituals). Unfortunately, not all patients can tolerate behavior therapy because of encompassing anxiety. Clearly, the behavior approaches need to be altered in dealing with the impulsive end of the spectrum.

Selected Readings

American Psychiatric Association: *Diagnostic and Statistical Manual of Mental Disorders,* 4th ed. Washington, DC, American Psychiatric Association, 1994.

Andreasen NC, Bardach J: Dysmorphophobia: symptom or disease? *Am J Psychiatry* 1977;134:673-676.

Anthony DT, Hollander E: Sexual compulsions. In: Hollander E, ed. *Obsessive Compulsive Related Disorders.* Washington, DC, American Psychiatric Press, 1993.

Aronowitz BA, Hollander E, DeCaria CM, et al: Neuropsychology of obsessive-compulsive disorder. *Neuropsychiatry Neuropsychol Behav Neurol* 1994;7:81-86.

Baer L: Factor analysis of symptom subtypes of obsessive compulsive disorder and their relation to personality and tic disorders. *J Clin Psychiatry* 1994;55:18-23.

Braddock LE: Dysmorphophobia in adolescence: a case report. *Br J Psychiatry* 1982;140:199-201.

Coleman E: Sexual compulsivity: definition, etiology, and treatment considerations. In: Coleman E, ed. *Chemical Dependency and Intimacy Dysfunction.* New York, NY, Hawarth Press, 1987.

DeCaria CM, Hollander E: Pathological gambling. In: Hollander E, ed. *Obsessive Compulsive Related Disorders.* Washington, DC, American Psychiatric Press, 1993.

Degonda M, Wyss M, Angst J: The Zurich Study. XVIII. Obsessive-compulsive disorder and syndromes in the general population. *Eur Arch Psychiatry Clin Neurosci* 1993;243:16-22.

Dominguez RA, Mestre SM: Management of treatment-refractory obsessive compulsive disorder patients. *J Clin Psychiatry* 1994;55: 86-92.

Emmanuel NP, Lydiard RB, Ballenger JC: Fluoxetine treatment of voyeurism. *Am J Psychiatry* 1991;148:950.

Fallon BA, Liebowitz MR, Salman E, et al: Fluoxetine for hypochondriacal patients without major depression. *J Clin Psychopharmacol* 1993;13:438-441.

Favazza AR: Repetitive self-mutilation. *Psychiatr Ann* 1992; 22:60-63.

Ford CV: Dimensions of somatization and hypochondriasis. *Neurol Clin* 1995;13:241-253.

Goodman WK, McDougle CJ, Price JH: Pharmacotherapy of obsessive-compulsive disorder. *J Clin Psychiatry* 1992;53:29-37.

Goodman WK, Price LH, Delgado PL, et al: Specificity of serotonin reuptake inhibitors in the treatment of obsessive-compulsive disorder. Comparison of fluvoxamine and desipramine. *Arch Gen Psychiatry* 1990;47:577-585.

Gwirtsman HE, Guze BH, Yager J, et al: Fluoxetine treatment of anorexia nervosa: an open clinical trial. *J Clin Psychiatry* 1990; 51:378-382.

Hollander E, Cohen L, Simeon D, et al: Fluvoxamine treatment of body dysmorphic disorder. *J Clin Psychopharmacol* 1994;14:75-77.

Hollander E, Cohen L, Simeon D: Body dysmorphic disorder. *Psychiatr Ann* 1993;3:359-364.

Hollander E, DeCaria CM, Nitescu A, et al: Serotonergic function in obsessive-compulsive disorder. Behavioral and neuroendocrine responses to oral m-chlorophenylpiperazine and fenfluramine in patients and healthy volunteers. *Arch Gen Psychiatry* 1992;49: 21-28.

Hollander E, Frenkel M, DeCaria C, et al: Treatment of pathological gambling with clomipramine. *Am J Psychiatry* 1992;149: 710-711.

Hollander E, Liebowitz MR, DeCaria C, et al: Treatment of depersonalization with serotonin reuptake blockers. *J Clin Psychopharmacol* 1990;10:200-203.

Hollander E, Liebowitz MR, Winchel R, et al: Treatment of body-dysmorphic disorder with serotonin reuptake blockers. *Am J Psychiatry* 1989;146:768-770.

Hollander E, Schiffman E, Cohen B, et al: Signs of central nervous system dysfunction in obsessive-compulsive disorder. *Arch Gen Psychiatry* 1990;47:27-32.

Hollander E, Wong CM: Body dysmorphic disorder, pathological gambling, and sexual compulsions. *J Clin Psychiatry* 1995;56:7-12.

Hollander E, Wong CM: Obsessive-compulsive spectrum disorders. *J Clin Psychiatry* 1995;56:3-6.

Hollander E, Wong CM: Spectrum, boundary, and subtyping issues: implications for treatment refractory obsessive-compulsive disorders. In: Goodman WK, Rudorfer MV, Maser JD, eds. *Obsessive-Compulsive Disorder: Contemporary Issues in Treatment.* Mahwah, NJ, Lawrence Erlbaum, 1999.

Hollander E: *Obsessive Compulsive Related Disorders.* Washington, DC, American Psychiatric Press, 1993.

Hollander E: Obsessive-compulsive spectrum disorders: an overview. *Psychiatr Ann* 1993;23:355-358.

Hollingsworth CE, Tanguay PE, Grossman L, et al: Long-term outcome of obsessive-compulsive disorder in childhood. *J Am Acad Child Psychiatry* 1980;19:134-144.

Holzer JC, Goodman WK, McDougle CJ, et al: Obsessive-compulsive disorder with and without a chronic tic disorder. A comparison of symptoms in 70 patients. *Br J Psychiatry* 1994;164: 469-473.

Hsu LK, Kaye W, Weltzin T: Are the eating disorders related to obsessive compulsive disorder? *Int J Eat Disord* 1993;14:305-318.

Kafka MP: Successful treatment of paraphilic coercive disorder (a rapist) with fluoxetine hydrochloride. *Br J Psychiatry* 1991;158: 844-847.

Leonard HL, Topol D, Bukstein O, et al: Clonazepam as an augmenting agent in the treatment of childhood-onset obsessive-compulsive disorder. *J Am Acad Child Adolesc Psychiatry* 1994;33: 792-794.

Lewis MH, Bodfish JW, Powell SB, et al: Clomipramine treatment for stereotype and related repetitive movement disorders associated with mental retardation. *Am J Ment Retard* 1995;100: 299-312.

McDougle CJ, Fleischmann RL, Epperson CN, et al: Risperidone addition in fluvoxamine-refractory obsessive-compulsive disorder: three cases. *J Clin Psychiatry* 1995;56:526-528.

McDougle CJ, Goodman WK, Leckman JF, et al: Haloperidol addition in fluvoxamine-refractory obsessive-compulsive disorder. A double-blind, placebo-controlled study in patients with and without tics. *Arch Gen Psychiatry* 1994;51:302-308.

McDougle CJ, Goodman WK, Price LH: Dopamine antagonists in tic-related and psychotic spectrum obsessive compulsive disorder. *J Clin Psychiatry* 1994;55:24-31.

McDougle CJ, Kresch LE, Goodman WK, et al: A case-controlled study of repetitive thoughts and behavior in adults with autistic disorder and obsessive-compulsive disorder. *Am J Psychiatry* 1995;152:772-777.

McElroy SL, Harrison GP, Keck PE, et al: Disorders of impulse control. In: Hollander E, Stein DJ, eds. *Impulsivity and Aggression.* John Wiley & Sons Ltd, 1995, pp 109-136.

McElroy SL, Keck PE Jr, Phillips KA: Kleptomania, compulsive buying, and binge-eating disorder. *J Clin Psychiatry* 1995;56:14-26.

McElroy SL, Keck PE Jr, Pope HG Jr, et al: Compulsive buying: a report of 20 cases. *J Clin Psychiatry* 1994;55:242-248.

McElroy SL, Pope HG Jr, Hudson JI, et al: Kleptomania: a report of 20 cases. *Am J Psychiatry* 1991;148:652-657.

Nicolini H, Weissbecker K, Mejia JM, et al: Family study of obsessive-compulsive disorder in a Mexican population. *Arch Med Res* 1993;24:193-198.

Pauls DL, Alsobrook JP 2nd, Goodman W, et al: A family study of obsessive-compulsive disorder. *Am J Psychiatry* 1995;152:76-84.

Phillips KA: Body dysmorphic disorder: the distress of imagined ugliness. *Am J Psychiatry* 1991;148:1138-1149.

Pigott TA, L'Heureux F, Hill JL, et al: A double-blind study of adjuvant buspirone hydrochloride in clomipramine-treated patients with obsessive-compulsive disorder. *J Clin Psychopharmacol* 1992;12:11-18.

Rosenthal RJ: Pathological gambling. *Psychiatr Ann* 1992;22: 72-78.

Stein DJ, Hollander E, Anthony DT, et al: Serotonergic medications for sexual obsessions, sexual addictions, and paraphilias. *J Clin Psychiatry* 1992;53:267-271.

Stein DJ, Mullen L, Islam MN, et al: Compulsive and impulsive symptomatology in trichotillomania. *Psychopathology* 1995;28: 208-213.

Swedo SE, Leonard HL: Childhood movement disorders and obsessive compulsive disorder. *J Clin Psychiatry* 1994;55:32-37.

Swedo SE, Leonard HL, Rapoport JL, et al: A double-blind comparison of clomipramine and desipramine in the treatment of trichotillomania. *N Engl J Med* 1989;321:491-501.

Swedo SE, Rapoport JL, Cheslow DL, et al: High prevalence of obsessive-compulsive symptoms in patients with Sydenham's chorea. *Am J Psychiatry* 1989;146:246-249.

Thiel A, Broocks A, Ohlmeier M, et al: Obsessive-compulsive disorder among patients with anorexia nervosa and bulimia nervosa. *Am J Psychiatry* 1995;152:72-75.

Thoren P, Asberg M, Bertilsson L, et al: Clomipramine treatment of obsessive-compulsive disorder. II. Biochemical aspects. *Arch Gen Psychiatry* 1980;37:1289-1294.

Warwick HM: Assessment of hypochondriasis. *Behav Res Ther* 1995;33:845-853.

Winchel RM: Trichotillomania: presentation and treatment. *Psychiatr Ann* 1992;22:84-89.

Wong CM, Hollander E: New dimensions in the OCD spectrum: autism, pathological gambling, and compulsive buying. *Primary Psychiatry* 1996;3:20-34.

Zohar J, Mueller EA, Insel TR, et al: Serotonergic responsivity in obsessive-compulsive disorder. Comparison of patients and healthy controls. *Arch Gen Psychiatry* 1987;44:946-951.

Chapter **15**

Posttraumatic Stress Disorder

Posttraumatic stress disorder (PTSD) was first introduced as a diagnostic category in part because of the increasing recognition of posttraumatic conditions in Vietnam War veterans. The central feature of PTSD is the development of characteristic symptoms after exposure to an extreme trauma. This can entail either personal or witnessed experience of an event that involves actual or threatened death or serious injury to self or others, or learning about expected or violent death, serious harm, or threat of death or injury experienced by a family member or close associate. The symptoms of PTSD involve persistent reexperiencing of the trauma, avoidance, hyperarousal, and numbing of responsiveness. The full syndrome lasts for at least 1 month, and can be caused by an acute stressor (duration less than 3 months) or a chronic stressor (duration of 3 months or longer). There can also be a delayed onset of symptoms that occurs at least 6 months after the traumatic event.

Studies of at-risk individuals have yielded prevalence rates ranging from 3% to 58%. PTSD may be found in up to 30% of disaster victims. Long-term physical effects have been documented in persons 30 years after having survived concentration camps. PTSD in the general population ranges from 1% to 14%. The Epidemiologic Catchment Area study found the lifetime prevalence of PTSD was 1%, with a rate of 0.5% in men and 1.3% in women. Another community survey of young adults found the lifetime prevalence of PTSD to be 9.2%, with a prevalence of 11.3% in women and 6% in men. The nature of the precipitating trauma also differed between the sexes. Combat and witnessing someone's death or injury were the principal traumas identified by men, and physical attack or threat accounted for more than half the traumas experienced by women.

PTSD patients have significant functioning difficulties, such as social function at work and personal relationships. Some studies have found the degree and severity of relationship stress in PTSD victims to be correlated to the severity of PTSD symptoms. However, in other studies, the degree and long-term disability of PTSD patients have been found to be more related to depressive symptoms rather than to the severity of PTSD itself.

Quality-of-life issues and morbidity from PTSD are significant. Gulf War veterans with PTSD had higher rates of psychiatric disorders (depression, anxiety, alcohol and substance abuse, sexual and cognitive dysfunction) and medical disorders (asthma, chronic fatigue, fibromyalgia), compared with veterans who had not seen combat. In addition, PTSD victims were more likely to be unemployed.

PTSD victims can include war veterans who have participated in torture and murder of other soldiers or civilians; survivors of aircraft and natural disasters; rape victims; Holocaust survivors; and cancer victims. The traumatic event can be reexperienced in various ways. Most commonly, the patient experiences intrusive and recurrent recollections of the event or a replaying of the event in dreams. Dissociation can occur, in some cases lasting from seconds to days, during which the patient behaves as though reliving the event. Severe distress occurs when the patient is exposed to stimuli that symbolize the traumatic event, such as anniversaries, hot humid weather (for Vietnam veterans), and uniformed guards (for Holocaust survivors). PTSD patients also avoid anything associated with the trauma, such as people, activities, or situations. This avoidance may be experienced as amnesia for a specific period during the event. Psychic numbing also occurs in this population, whereby patients feel detached and estranged with anhedonia and decreased ability to feel emotions. Symptoms of hyperarousal experienced by PTSD victims include sleeping difficulties, increased startle response, hypervigilance, difficulty concentrating, and increased irritability.

Beyond the core symptoms of PTSD, there seem to be enduring changes in patients' personality after chronic trauma. These include a lasting change in the person's sense of identity and interpersonal relationships, and the sense of life's meaning. Besides prominent anxiety, PTSD patients also experience significant depression and dissociation. Other symptoms include survivor guilt, panic attacks, shame, frustrated helplessness, and rage. There may be periods of impulsivity, aggression, or explosive behavior. PTSD patients may experience somatic complaints and feelings of ineffectiveness, as well as hallucinations and delusions.

PTSD can occur at any age, including childhood. Symptoms usually begin in the first 3 months after the trauma, although, with a delayed onset, symptoms might not appear until years after the event. Catastrophe victims often tend to have a delayed onset of PTSD. For the most part, PTSD patients meet criteria for acute stress disorder immediately after the event. Half of those patients, however, experience a resolution of symptoms within 3 months with appropriate treatment. Three stages of PTSD have been described by Scrignar. Stage one involves the response to the trauma. Stage two (acute PTSD) occurs when the symptoms persist more than 4 weeks. During this stage, feelings of helplessness, loss of control, hyperarousal, reliving of the trauma, phobic avoidance, exaggerated startle response, and somatic symptoms may occur. Stage three is described as chronic PTSD, when the patient changes focus from the actual trauma to the physical disability caused by the trauma. During this stage, substance abuse, anxiety, and depression are common complicating factors. A history of affective disorder is a risk factor for the development of PTSD in women, and a history of anxiety disorder and parental mental disorder are risk factors for the development of PTSD in men.

Regarding comorbid psychiatric illness, PTSD patients face an increased risk for the development of panic disorder, agoraphobia, OCD, phobias, major depressive disorder, somatization disorder, and substance-related disorders. PTSD patients with melancholic depressive disorders have been found to have severe emotional numbing. Women were also found to be more susceptible to developing panic disorders and phobias compared to men. PTSD patients are also at increased risk for self-mutilatory behavior and suicides. PTSD patients with depressive comorbidity have a higher frequency of suicidal thoughts, and nondepressive PTSD patients have an increased frequency of suicide attempts. In addition, among the patients with PTSD who manifested suicidality, the suicide method used in ideation or attempts was found to be associated with the type of trauma the patients were exposed to. For example, torture victims who experienced blunt force to their head and body were found to have suicidal behavior involving jumping from a height or from a train, water torture was associated with drowning, and sharp-force torture was associated with self-inflicted stabbing or cutting. Also, asthma is a common medical comorbidity in adolescent PTSD victims.

Case Report

FT was a 34-year-old, single, white male who sought treatment because he was experiencing washing rituals and intrusive thoughts about AIDS, extreme anxiety, and

Table 1: Differential Diagnoses of Posttraumatic Stress Disorder

- Adjustment disorder, in which the stressor can be of any severity compared to the life-threatening stressor experienced in PTSD

- Acute stress disorder, in which the symptoms are limited to a 4-week period

- OCD, in which the recurrent intrusive thoughts are inappropriate and are not related to an experienced traumatic event

- Schizophrenia and other psychotic disorders, in which perceptual difficulties such as hallucinations and delusions are experienced and should be differentiated from flashbacks in PTSD, and there is not an associated life-threatening stressor preceding the development of symptoms

- Mood disorders with psychotic features, in which there is no precipitating life-threatening stressor preceding the development of depressive symptoms

- Delirium, in which there is waxing and waning of the sensorium

- Substance-induced disorders

- Psychotic disorders caused by a general medical condition

- Malingering, which should be ruled out when financial benefits and forensic determinations are involved

sleep disturbances. He said that the symptoms had lasted for years, but recently had gotten much worse. The intrusive thoughts and rituals started in his 20s and had increased in severity. He had been tested for HIV numerous times and found to be negative. He also described symptoms of hyperarousal, such as sleep disturbance, irritability, exaggerated startle response, and difficulty concentrating. He did not exhibit any other signs or symptoms of depression. He had recently lost a job because he could not attend to his duties as a salesman. He was started on a trial of fluoxetine (Prozac®). After several months of treatment, the washing rituals and intrusive thoughts abated somewhat, but he continued to have significant anxiety, distress, and hyperarousal symptoms. After much probing, the patient finally volunteered that he was date raped in his late teens, and since then had developed these symptoms, was too ashamed to tell anyone, and felt that it was all his fault. He also admitted to reexperiencing the trauma, as well as avoidance and numbing. He was referred to group psychotherapy while continuing on his medication. He continues to improve with treatment.

Differential diagnoses of PTSD are listed in Table 1.

Treatment

Treatment of PTSD in the general clinical setting often involves a combination of pharmacotherapy, supportive psychotherapy, cognitive-behavior therapy, and psychoeducation, although specialized clinics may use more targeted and tailored treatment for special populations of trauma victims. In pharmacotherapy, the usual approach is to start with an antidepressant that is effective against both the numbing and intrusive symptoms. Selective serotonin reuptake inhibitors (SSRIs), monoamine oxidase inhibitors (MAOIs), and tricyclic antidepressants (TCAs) are often used, in that order. A positive response to antidepressants results in 60% to 70% of cases. Moreover, antidepressants have been found to have a positive impact on psychotherapy in 70% of cases. Treatment trials should last at least 12 weeks. The global response at weeks 2 or 4 of treatment is a better indicator of eventual treatment response for fluoxetine, an SSRI, but not for amitriptyline (Elavil®), a TCA.

Several SSRIs have been shown to be helpful in the treatment of PTSD. Fluoxetine in dosage ranges of 20 to 80 mg/d has been shown to improve symptoms of hyperarousal, reexperiencing, and avoidance/numbing. Paroxetine (Paxil®) has been shown to be effective in the treatment of all three PTSD symptom clusters of numbing, intrusive thoughts, and hyperarousal. Sertraline (Zoloft®) was recently approved and is the only drug or SSRI indicated for PTSD. Fluvoxamine (Luvox®) may also be useful. Traditional MAOIs such as phenelzine (Nardil®) in dosage ranges of 45 to 75 mg/d have been found helpful in those patients with predominantly intrusive symptoms, with an improvement of 60% in that symptom cluster. Moclobemide, a reversible MAO-A inhibitor, also seems promising for the treatment of PTSD. Tricyclic antidepressants such as imipramine (Tofranil®) in dosage ranges of 50 to 350 mg/d, and desipramine (Norpramin®) have been shown to improve PTSD symptoms. However, other studies have not shown positive treatment results of core symptoms of PTSD with amitriptyline or desipramine when compared to placebo.

Benzodiazepines such as alprazolam (Xanax®) have been found to be less effective over time, although they are useful in acute situations to target anxiety and hyperarousal, not necessarily the other core symptoms of PTSD such as numbing and intrusive thoughts. Clonazepam (Klonopin®) may be more useful than the other benzodiazepines because of its serotonergic properties. In addition, rebound effects are common when the benzodiazepines are discontinued.

Less commonly used agents include beta-blockers such as propranolol (Inderal®) in dosages up to 160 mg/d, and clonidine (Catapres®), an alpha-$_2$ (nonadrenergic) antagonist, in the dosage range of 0.2 to 0.4 mg/d to target hyperarousal symptoms. Adrenergic blockers are useful as augmentation to antidepressants in PTSD.

Mood stabilizers are another group of medications that can be used to target symptoms of impulsivity and irritability in the PTSD population. These medications include lithium, valproate (Depakote®), and carbamazepine (Tegretol®). Other medications include trazodone (Desyrel®), which may be helpful in the treatment of PTSD and sleep disturbances associated with it. Buspirone (BuSpar®) may also be helpful, especially to target anxiety symptoms. A novel psychotropic, brofaromine (a combined MAO-A inhibitor/serotonin transport inhibitor), is also being studied for the treatment of PTSD.

Selected Readings

American Psychiatric Association: *Diagnostic and Statistical Manual of Mental Disorders*, 4th ed. Washington, DC, American Psychiatric Association, 1994.

Bleich A, Siegel B, Garb R, et al: Post-traumatic stress disorder following combat exposure: clinical features and psychopharmacological treatment. *Br J Psychiatry* 1986;149:365-369.

Brady KT, Sonne SC, Roberts JM: Sertraline treatment of comorbid posttraumatic stress disorder and alcohol dependence. *J Clin Psychiatry* 1995;56:502-505.

Braun P, Greenberg D, Dasberg H, et al: Core symptoms of posttraumatic stress disorder unimproved by alprazolam treatment. *J Clin Psychiatry* 1990;51:236-238.

Breslau N, Davis GC, Andreski P, et al: Traumatic events and posttraumatic stress disorder in an urban population of young adults. *Arch Gen Psychiatry* 1991;48:216-222.

Bromet E, Sonnega A, Kessler RC: Risk factors for DSM-III-R posttraumatic stress disorder: findings from the National Comorbidity Survey. *Am J Epidemiol* 1998;147:353-361.

Burstein A: Treatment length in post-traumatic stress disorder. *Psychosomatics* 1986;27:632-637.

Burstein A: Treatment of post-traumatic stress disorder with imipramine. *Psychosomatics* 1984;25:681-687.

Butler RW, Mueser KT, Sprock J, et al: Positive symptoms of psychosis in posttraumatic stress disorder. *Biol Psychiatry* 1996;39:839-844.

Chapman D: A brief introduction to contemporary disaster research. In: Boher G, Chapman D, eds. *Man and Society in Disaster*. New York, Basic Books, 1962.

Constans JI, Lenhoff K, McCarthy M: Depression subtyping in PTSD patients. *Ann Clin Psychiatry* 1997;9:235-240.

Davidson J, Kudler H, Smith R, et al: Treatment of posttraumatic stress disorder with amitriptyline and placebo. *Arch Gen Psychiatry* 1990;47:259-266.

Davidson JR, Malik ML, Sutherland SN: Response characteristics to antidepressants and placebo in post-traumatic stress disorder. *Int Clin Psychopharmacol* 1997;12:291-296.

Davidson JR, Weisler RH, Malik M, et al: Fluvoxamine in civilians with posttraumatic stress disorder. *J Clin Psychopharmacol* 1998;18:93-95.

Duffy JD, Malloy PF: Efficacy of buspirone in the treatment of posttraumatic stress disorder: an open trial. *Ann Clin Psychiatry* 1994;6:33-37.

Eitinger L: Organic and psychosomatic after effects of concentration camp imprisonment. *Inter Psychiatry Clinic* 1971;8:205-215.

Ferrada-Noli M, Asberg M, Ormstad K, et al: Suicidal behavior after severe trauma. Part 1: PTSD diagnoses, psychiatric comorbidity, and assessments of suicidal behavior. *J Trauma Stress* 1998;11:103-112.

Ferrada-Noli M, Asberg M, Ormstad K: Suicidal behavior after severe trauma. Part 2: The association between methods of torture and of suicidal ideation in posttraumatic stress disorder. *J Trauma Stress* 1998;11:113-124.

Fesler FA: Valproate in combat-related posttraumatic stress disorder. *J Clin Psychiatry* 1991;52:361-364.

Ford N: The use of anticonvulsants in posttraumatic stress disorder: case study and overview. *J Trauma Stress* 1996;9:857-863.

Forster PL, Schoenfeld FB, Marmar CR, et al: Lithium for irritability in post-traumatic stress disorder. *J Trauma Stress* 1995;8: 143-149.

Frank JB, Kosten TR, Giller EL Jr, et al: A randomized clinical trial of phenelzine and imipramine for posttraumatic stress disorder. *Am J Psychiatry* 1988;145:1289-1291.

Helzer JE, Robins LN, McEvoy L: Post-traumatic stress disorder in the general population. Findings of the epidemiologic catchment area survey. *N Engl J Med* 1987;317:1630-1634.

Herman JL, Perry JC, van der Kolk BA: Childhood trauma in borderline personality disorder. *Am J Psychiatry* 1989;146:490-495.

Hertzberg MA, Feldman ME, Beckham JC, et al: Trial of trazodone for posttraumatic stress disorder using a multiple baseline group design. *J Clin Psychopharmacol* 1996;16:294-298.

Hollander E, Simeon D, Gorman JM: Anxiety disorders. In: Hales RE, Yudofsky SC, Talbott JA, eds. *American Psychiatric Press Textbook of Psychiatry*, 2nd ed. Washington DC, American Psychiatric Press, 1994.

Iowa Persian Gulf Study Group: Self-reported illness and health status among Gulf War veterans. A population-based study. *JAMA* 1997;277:238-245.

Katz L, Fleisher W, Kjernisted K, et al: A review of the psychobiology and pharmacotherapy of posttraumatic stress disorder. *Can J Psychiatry* 1996;41:233-238.

Katz RJ, Lott MH, Arbus P, et al: Pharmacotherapy of post-traumatic stress disorder with a novel psychotropic. *Anxiety* 1994; 1:169-174.

Kauffman CD, Reist C, Djenderedjian A, et al: Biological markers of affective disorders and posttraumatic stress disorder: a pilot study with desipramine. *J Clin Psychiatry* 1987;48:366-367.

Kinzie JD, Leung P: Clonidine in Cambodian patients with posttraumatic stress disorder. *J Nerv Ment Dis* 1989;177:546-550.

Kolb LC, Burris BC, Griffiths S: Propranolol and clonidine in treatment of the chronic post-traumatic stress disorders of war. In: van der Kolk BA, ed. *Post-Traumatic Stress Disorder: Psychological and Biological Sequelae*. Washington, DC, American Psychiatric Press, 1984.

Koltek M, Wilkes TC, Atkinson M: The prevalence of posttraumatic stress disorder in an adolescent inpatient unit. *Can J Psychiatry* 1998;43:64-68.

Looff D, Grimley P, Kuller F, et al: Carbamazepine for PTSD. *J Am Acad Child Adolesc Psychiatry* 1995;34:703-704.

Marshall RD, Schneier FR, Fallon BA, et al: An open trial of paroxetine in patients with noncombat-related, chronic posttraumatic stress disorder. *J Clin Psychopharmacol* 1998;18:10-18.

Nagy LM, Morgan CA 3d, Southwick SM, et al: Open prospective trial of fluoxetine for posttraumatic stress disorder. *J Clin Psychopharmacol* 1993;13:107-113.

Neal LA, Shapland W, Fox C: An open trial of moclobemide in the treatment of post-traumatic stress disorder. *Int Clin Psychopharmacol* 1997;12:231-237.

Reist C, Kauffmann CD, Haier RJ, et al: A controlled trial of desipramine in 18 men with posttraumatic stress disorder. *Am J Psychiatry* 1989;146:513-516.

Riggs DS, Byrne CA, Weathers FW, et al: The quality of the intimate relationships of male Vietnam veterans: problems associated with posttraumatic stress disorder. *J Trauma Stress* 1998;11:87-101.

Scrignar CB: *Post-Traumatic Stress Disorder: Diagnosis, Treatment, and Legal Issues.* New York, Praeger, 1984.

Sims A, Sims D: The phenomenology of post-traumatic stress disorder. A symptomatic study of 70 victims of psychological trauma. *Psychopathology* 1998;31:96-112.

Sutherland SM, Davidson JR: Pharmacotherapy for post-traumatic stress disorder. *Psychiatr Clin North Am* 1994;17:409-423.

Tucker W: Recognition and management of posttraumatic stress disorder: approaches for the practitioner. *J Pract Psychiatry Behav Health* 1998;4:20-27.

van der Kolk BA, Dreyfuss D, Michaels M, et al: Fluoxetine in posttraumatic stress disorder. *J Clin Psychiatry* 1994;55:517-522.

van der Kolk BA, Saporta J: The biological response to psychic trauma: mechanisms and treatment of intrusion and numbing. *Anxiety Res* 1991;4:199-212.

Zatzick DF, Weiss DS, Marmar CR, et al: Post-traumatic stress disorder and functioning and quality of life outcomes in female Vietnam veterans. *Mil Med* 1997;162:661-665.

Chapter **16**

Refractory Anxiety

Most patients with anxiety disorders can be effectively treated with specific pharmacologic and psychotherapeutic approaches. Nevertheless, some anxiety patients remain refractory to standard treatments. For these patients, reappraisal and a systematic approach to treatment can be helpful.

Common problems in patients who are treatment resistant are an inadequate dosage or an inadequate duration of medication treatment. Alternatively, the diagnosis may need to be reconsidered and new diagnoses entertained since the initial consultation. Comorbid diagnoses should also be carefully assessed. Comorbid psychiatric, medical, and neurologic conditions may complicate treatment of anxiety or require additional specific treatments. Depression and substance abuse are especially likely to complicate anxiety disorders. In addition, personality disorders increase the resistance to treatment and must be addressed through psychotherapy. Also, a number of medications and conditions can produce anxiety symptoms (see Chapter 9). Clinicians should evaluate patients for hyperthyroidism, chronic obstructive pulmonary disease, and physiologic sequelae of drug, alcohol, and over-the-counter medication abuse. Finally, alternative pharmacologic and biologic approaches for specific types of anxiety can yield successful outcomes.

When considering augmentation strategies in treating anxiety disorders, clinicians should look at the specific

Table 1: General Principles in Treatment of Refractory Anxiety

Symptom Cluster	Medication
Cognitive/apprehensive expectation	SSRI
Autonomic symptoms	beta-blocker
Social anxiety	MAOI (not in combination with an SSRI)
Alcohol/substance abuse	avoid benzodiazepines
Anticipatory anxiety	benzodiazepine or buspirone (BuSpar®)
Phobic avoidance	benzodiazepines, MAOI, or behavior therapy
Depression	SSRI, tricyclic antidepressant (TCA), MAOI, or serotonin-norepinephrine reuptake inhibitor (SNRI)

anxiety symptom clusters and comorbid psychiatric illness to guide the selection of the best agent.

General principles regarding strategies for treatment-resistant anxiety disorders based on symptom clusters are summarized in Table 1.

For example, if a patient has panic disorder, the acute panic attack may be treated with: (1) high-potency benzodiazepines such as alprazolam (Xanax®) or clonazepam (Klonopin®); (2) a tricyclic antidepressant (TCA), to a maximum of the equivalent of 250 mg/d of imipramine

Table 2: Principles for Augmentation Strategies

- Depression: add antidepressant such as SSRI, TCA, SNRI, MAOI (do not combine an MAOI with other serotonergic medications like the SSRIs, SNRIs, clomipramine [Anafranil®], and buspirone [BuSpar®])

- Impulse control disorders: add a mood stabilizer such as lithium (Lithobid®), or anticonvulsants such as valproate (Depakote®), carbamazepine (Tegretol®), gabapentin (Neurontin®), or lamotrigine (Lamictal®)

- Bipolar disorder: add a mood stabilizer

- Substantial anxiety: add buspirone (BuSpar®) or clonazepam (Klonopin®)

- Neurologic involvement: add an anticonvulsant

- Delusional and psychotic symptoms: add a neuroleptic

- Tics/Tourette's syndrome: add a neuroleptic such as pimozide (Orap®), haloperidol (Haldol®), olanzapine (Zyprexa®), or risperidone (Risperdal®)

- Comorbid borderline or antisocial personality disorder: mood stabilizer (eg, Lithobid®, Depakote®) for impulsive symptoms

(Tofranil®); or a selective serotonin reuptake inhibitor (SSRI) such as paroxetine (Paxil®), 40 to 50 mg/d, or sertraline (Zoloft®), 50 to 200 mg/d (starting dose 25 mg/d). For the anticipatory anxiety component of panic disorder, treatment can include buspirone (BuSpar®) or a benzodiazepine. Finally, for persistent phobic avoidance, treatment with behavior therapy, benzodiazepines, or a monoamine oxidase inhibitor (MAOI) may be used. Combination treatment with an MAOI and an SSRI should not be used, however.

In addition, combinations of medications may be necessary for patients with comorbid psychiatric disorders. Guiding principles to augmentation strategies are outlined in Table 2.

Clinicians must keep in mind that, when combining antidepressant medications, TCA levels are increased with concomitant SSRI use, thereby making careful titration essential, following blood levels to prevent toxicity. For example, when combining the TCA clomipramine (Anafranil®) with an SSRI such as fluoxetine (Prozac®), the dosage for clomipramine ranges from 50 to 100 mg/d, and that for fluoxetine is about 20 mg/d. The combined clomipramine and desmethylclomipramine levels should not exceed 800 ng/mL to minimize risk of seizures.

Certain treatments have *not* been shown to be helpful in the anxiety disorders. For generalized anxiety disorder, these include antipsychotic agents, barbiturates, opiates, antihistamines, and over-the-counter medications. For panic disorder, ineffective treatments include bupropion (Wellbutrin®), buspirone (BuSpar®), neuroleptics, beta-blockers, and electroconvulsive treatment.

Alternative treatment strategies for panic disorder may be indicated. These include the use of valproate (Depakote®) 500 to 3,000 mg/d, carbamazepine (Tegretol®) 400 to 1,200 mg/d, and verapamil (Calan®) 240 to 480 mg/d, all of which have been reported to be of some help to treatment-refractory patients.

For obsessive-compulsive disorder, additional treatments can be attempted for treatment-refractory patients, including neuroleptic augmentation with agents such as pimozide (Orap®), risperidone (Risperdal®), or inositol, intravenous clomipramine, antiandrogens, and neurosurgery, including capsulotomy and cingulotomy.

Case Report

LR was a 37-year-old, single, Italian Catholic female, unemployed and living at home with her family. She was diagnosed with OCD 15 years earlier. The patient described her current symptoms as "intense, unbearable, and stressful," comprised of constant obsessions of sins against saints and God, as well as cursing and blasphemy, rituals of sacrificing her food to atone for her sins, and repetitive cleaning rituals, all of which often took up the entire day. She would also often not sleep because she felt compelled to complete certain religious rituals. She also had major depression. She needed multiple hospitalizations over the years for her mental problems, particularly because of suicidality and significant weight loss from the ritualistic starvation (although she did not have anorexia). Her multiple suicide attempts included overdosing with pills, swallowing ammonia, and slitting her wrists. She had been placed on multiple pharmacotherapeutic regimens, including fluoxetine, clomipramine, fluvoxamine (Luvox®), paroxetine (Paxil®), sertraline (Zoloft®), phenelzine (Nardil®), and combination of an SSRI with risperidone, clonazepam (Klonopin®), valproate, and lithium (Lithobid®), all with minimal improvement of symptoms. She also underwent a course of electroconvulsive therapy (ECT), which did not help. She tried cognitive-behavior therapy, but was too anxious. She had a family history significant for bipolar disorder in her father, and depression and OCD in her mother and brother. She was eventually referred for neurosurgery. She underwent a cingulotomy while being maintained on a regimen of sertraline (200 mg/d) and lithium (300 mg b.i.d.). Preoperative positron emission tomography (PET) scans showed significant hypofrontality and increased activity of the cingulate gyrus. The patient had some improvement in both the OCD and depressive symptoms up to 6 months postoperatively. Her postoperative PET scan showed normalization of cingulate gyrus activity but no improvement in the hypofrontality. Unfortunately, she relapsed and has been managed on multiple medication regimens with minimal improvement of symptoms. She was unwilling to undergo a second cingulotomy.

Treatment of anxiety disorders in patients with comorbid mood disorders should also be addressed. About 85% of all depressed patients experience significant symptoms of anxiety. Similarly, comorbid depression occurs in up to 90% of patients with anxiety disorders. Antidepressant medications—including the SSRIs, SNRIs, TCAs, and MAOIs—are highly effective in the management of comorbid depression and anxiety. Acute use of benzodiazepines may be necessary because of a lag time of up to 6 weeks for the antidepressant/antianxiety effects of the antidepressant used. Cognitive and behavior therapy should also be used.

Selected Readings

Baetz M, Bowen RC: Efficacy of divalproex sodium in patients with panic disorder and mood instability who have not responded to conventional therapy. *Can J Psychiatry* 1998;43:73-77.

Coplan JD, Gorman JM: Treatment of anxiety disorder in patients with mood disorders. *J Clin Psychiatry* 1990;51:9-13.

Coplan JD, Tiffon L, Gorman JM: Therapeutic strategies for the patient with treatment-resistant anxiety. *J Clin Psychiatry* 1993; 54:69-74.

Fallon BA, Campeas R, Schneier FR, et al: Open trial of intravenous clomipramine in five treatment-refractory patients with obsessive-compulsive disorder. *J Neuropsychiatry Clin Neurosci* 1992;4:70-75.

Gorman JM: Comorbid depression and anxiety spectrum disorders. *Depress Anxiety* 1996;4:160-168.

Hollander E, Cohen LJ: The assessment and treatment of refractory anxiety. *J Clin Psychiatry* 1994;55:27-31.

Hollander E, Simeon D, Gorman JM: Anxiety disorders. In: Hales RE, Yudofsky SC, Talbott JA, eds. *American Psychiatric Press Textbook of Psychiatry*, 2nd ed. Washington, DC, American Psychiatric Press, 1994.

Hollander E, Wong CM: Developments in the treatment of obsessive-compulsive disorder. *Primary Psychiatry* 1995;Feb:28-33.

Jenike MA, Baer L, Ballantine T, et al: Cingulotomy for refractory obsessive-compulsive disorder. A long-term follow-up of 33 patients. *Arch Gen Psychiatry* 1991;48:548-555.

Keck PE Jr, McElroy SL, Tugrul KC, et al: Antiepileptic drugs for the treatment of panic disorder. *Neuropsychobiology* 1993;27:150-153.

Klein E, Uhde TW: Controlled study of verapamil for treatment of panic disorder. *Am J Psychiatry* 1988;145:431-434.

Kuzel RJ: Treating comorbid depression and anxiety. *J Fam Pract* 1996;43:S45-S53.

McDougle CJ, Goodman WK, Price LH, et al: Neuroleptic addition in fluvoxamine-refractory obsessive-compulsive disorder. *Am J Psychiatry* 1990;147:652-654.

Saxena S, Wang D, Bystritsky A, et al: Risperidone augmentation of SRI treatment for refractory obsessive-compulsive disorder. *J Clin Psychiatry* 1996;57:303-306.

Index

A

abecarnil 110

abnormal orgasm 17

acetazolamide 64

acetylcholine 11, 12

acne 59, 64

Adalat® 27

addiction 32

adjustment disorder 49, 53, 71, 74, 76, 84, 109, 154

affective disorder 153

aggression 35

agitation 13, 26, 34, 45, 48, 49, 78, 97, 102, 131

agoraphobia 94, 104, 114, 115, 121-123, 153

agranulocytosis 17, 65, 66

AIDS 153

akathisia 15, 23

alcohol 9, 24, 25, 34, 35, 72, 79, 92, 97, 102, 108, 116, 120, 130, 151, 161, 162

alcoholism 7

alexithymia 77

alkalosis 114

allergic reactions 35

alopecia 65

alpha-adrenergic blockers 24

alprazolam (Xanax®) 30-33, 94, 110, 116, 117, 124, 156, 162

Alzheimer's disease 103

amantadine (Symmetrel®) 30

amitriptyline (Elavil®) 20-22, 110, 156

amnesia 152

amphetamines 25, 29, 95

Anafranil® 20, 130, 163, 164

angiotensin-converting enzyme (ACE) inhibitors 64, 104

anhedonia 44, 45, 51, 152

anorexia 14, 48, 52, 94, 109, 130, 137-139, 144, 165

anorgasmia 14, 27

Antabuse® 25, 35

antacids 34

B

barbiturates 25, 34, 36, 108, 164

benzodiazepines 18, 19, 24, 29, 31, 32, 34-37, 62, 67, 95, 98, 105, 110, 116, 133, 156, 163, 164, 166

bereavement 49, 53, 71, 73, 74, 76

beta-adrenergic blockers 24, 27, 62, 77, 98, 105, 123, 156, 162, 164

bifascicular block 23

binge eating 137, 138, 144

bipolar disorder 8, 49, 52, 53, 58-62, 65, 76, 163, 165

blood dyscrasias 66

blood urea nitrogen (BUN) 63

blurred vision 23, 68

blushing 120

body dysmorphic disorder (BDD) 102, 122, 130, 131, 137, 138, 142, 144

borderline personality disorder 52, 61, 72, 98, 143, 163

bradycardia 30

brain herniation 38

brain injury 84

breast-feeding 16, 35

brofaromine 157

bulimia 52, 137, 138

bupropion (Wellbutrin®, Wellbutrin® SR, Zyban®) 18, 19, 29, 30, 73, 80, 95, 96, 99, 164

BuSpar® 36, 95, 105, 110, 124, 143, 157, 162-164

buspirone (BuSpar®) 36, 56, 95, 97, 105, 110, 124, 133, 143, 157, 162-164

C

caffeine 18, 64, 104

Calan® 164

calcium 64

calcium-channel blockers 18, 19, 27, 29, 62, 94

cancer 9, 77, 84

cannabis 116

capsulotomy 133, 164

D

diuretics 15, 24, 26, 64

divorce 74

dizziness 13, 17, 34, 36, 66-68, 103, 105, 114

dopamine 12, 16, 56, 140

drowsiness 14

drug abuse 32

drug rash 65

dry mouth 17, 23, 29, 120

dysarthria 66

dyscontrol 35

dyspepsia 14

dysphoria 32, 46, 62

dyspnea 103

dysthymia 51, 53, 71-73, 76, 92, 121, 122

E

eating disorders 11, 51, 59, 94-96, 130, 137-139

Ebstein's anomaly 82

echolalia 48

echopraxia 48

edema 64

Effexor® XR 16, 110

Effexor® 16, 55, 83, 94, 95, 124

ejaculation 17

elatedness 47

Elavil® 20, 22, 110, 156

Eldepryl® 24

electrocardiogram (ECG) 22, 37, 63, 65, 77

electroconvulsive therapy (ECT) 36-38, 54, 62, 78, 79, 82, 83, 85-87, 95, 164, 165

emesis 23

enuresis 11

Equanil® 36

erythema multiforme 68

erythromycin 35, 67

Eskalith CR® 62, 63

Eskalith® 47, 56, 62, 95, 96

estrogen (Premarin®) 35, 83

ethosuximide (Zarontin®) 67

euphoria 35

exfoliative dermatitis 66

exhaustion 48

eyestrain 38

F

falls 78

fatigue 22, 35, 45, 67, 96, 103, 151

fenfluramine (Pondimin®) 143

fetal malformations 81

fibromyalgia 151

fingernail hypoplasia 82

Flagyl® 64

flesinoxan 111

flight of ideas 47

'floppy baby' syndrome 82

flumazenil (Romazicon®) 34

fluoxetine (Prozac®) 12-14, 16, 17, 19, 26, 29, 73, 80, 81, 83, 87, 94, 95, 98, 108, 110, 116, 124, 130, 132, 155, 156, 164, 165

fluvoxamine (Luvox®) 12, 14, 16, 18, 29, 80, 81, 116, 124, 132, 156, 165

folate 77

frontal lobe deficits 128

G

GABA-A 34

gabapentin (Neurontin®) 47, 62, 67, 163

gamma-aminobutyric acid (GABA) 11, 31, 141, 143

gastric lavage 23

gastrointestinal (GI) upset 13, 14, 36

generalized anxiety disorder (GAD) 6, 36, 102, 104, 107, 109, 110, 116, 122, 164

gepirone 111

glucocorticoids 25

grandiosity 47

group A beta-hemolytic streptococci 129

group therapy 84

guanethidine (Ismelin®) 24

guilt 45, 48, 73, 140, 142

H

Halcion® 32

Haldol® 143, 163

M

O

P

pain 6, 11, 51

palpitations 8, 103, 105, 120

Pamelor® 20, 22, 55, 85, 99, 143

pancreatitis 65

panic attacks 45, 49, 94, 104, 105, 108, 109, 113-115, 117, 120-122, 152, 162

panic disorder 6, 51, 95, 102, 104, 109, 113-116, 120-122, 130, 153, 162-164

paranoia 46, 98, 122

paraphilias 144

parathyroid disease 115

parathyroid hormone 64

paresthesias 105

parkinson-like movement disorders 15

parkinsonism 23

Parkinson's disease 77, 103

Parnate® 24, 26, 98, 123

paroxetine (Paxil®) 12, 14, 16, 17, 19, 80, 81, 85, 87, 94, 98, 110, 116, 122, 124, 132, 156, 163, 165

pathologic gambling 102, 138, 140, 142, 144

Paxil® 14, 16, 17, 19, 81, 94, 110, 116, 122, 132, 156, 163, 165

pediatric autoimmune neuropsychiatric disorders associated with streptococcal infections (PANDAS) 129

pentobarbital (Nembutal®) 36

performance anxiety 122

Periactin® 14

personality disorders 11, 35, 48, 52, 54, 72, 115, 161

phenelzine (Nardil®) 24, 26, 116, 123, 156, 165

phenobarbital 65, 68

phentolamine (Regitine®) 27

phenytoin (Dilantin®) 18, 19, 25, 30, 35, 65, 67, 68

U

urinalysis 77

urinary hesitancy 23

urinary retention 78

V

Valium® 30, 32-34

valproate (valproic acid, Depakene®, Depakote®, Depakote® Sprinkle) 47, 60, 62, 65-68, 82, 95, 97, 131, 157, 163-165

Venereal Disease Research Laboratory (VDRL) 77

venlafaxine (Effexor®, Effexor® XR) 12, 16, 55, 80, 83, 94, 95, 110, 124

verapamil (Calan®) 164

Versed® 32

vertigo 102, 103, 115

vestibular problems 116

Viagra® 14

violence 58

Visken® 95

visual disturbances 64

visual/spatial impairments 128

vitamin B_{12} 77

vitamin B_6 27

volume expansion 79

vomiting 13, 22, 27, 28, 34, 64, 65

W

warfarin (Coumadin®) 18, 19, 24, 66, 67

weakness 8, 35

weight change 45

weight gain 17, 23, 27, 46, 48, 49, 59, 64, 65, 67, 94, 109

weight loss 45, 48, 78, 94, 165

Wellbutrin® 18, 29, 95, 96, 164

Wellbutrin® SR 29, 30

withdrawal 22, 31, 32, 34-36, 80, 102, 110, 124

X

Xanax® 30-33, 94, 110,
116, 124, 156, 162

Xylocaine® 37

Y

Yocon® 14

yohimbine (Yocon®) 14

Z

Zarontin® 67

Zofran® 111

Zoloft® 14, 16, 17, 19,
73, 81, 94, 116, 132,
156, 163, 165

Zyban® 29, 30

Zyprexa® 62, 163